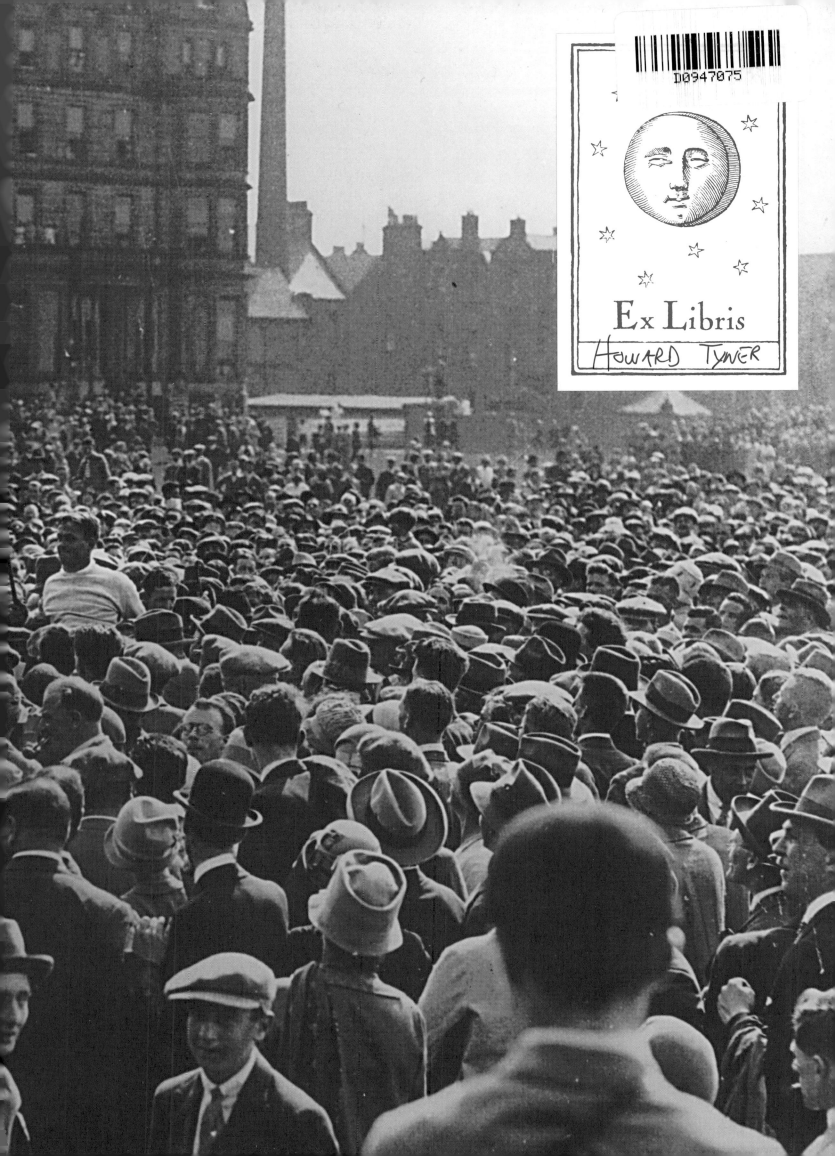

LIFE AND TIMES OF
BOBBY JONES

Sidney L. Matthew

With a Foreword by
Robert Tyre Jones IV

SLEEPING BEAR PRESS 1995

SLEEPING BEAR PRESS

ALL INQUIRIES SHOULD BE
ADDRESSED TO: SLEEPING BEAR PRESS
                                 121 South Main Street
                                 P.O. Box 20
                                 Chelsea, MI 48118

Grateful acknowledgments are made to the following publishing companies for permission to reprint various sentences and paragraphs: Random House, *The World of Golf,* Charles Price (1962); Alfred A. Knopf, *Farewell to Sport,* (1938, renewed 1966 by Paul Gallico); Doubleday & Company, Inc., *Golf Is My Game,* Robert Tyre Jones (1960); Doubleday & Company, Inc., *Bobby Jones on Golf,* Robert Tyre Jones (1966); Harpers, *The Boy's Life of Bobby Jones,* O.B. Keeler (1931); Holt Rinehart & Winston, *Triumphant Journey: The Saga of Bobby Jones and The Grand Slam of Golf,* Richard Miller (1980); and Minton Balch, *Down The Fairway: The Golf Life and Play of Robert T. Jones, Jr.,* Robert T. Jones, Jr. and O.B. Keeler (1927), copyright by JONESHEIRS INC.

The gold stamp on the cover is a line drawing of Bob Jones' last shot in competition – a mashie pitch to the 11th hole at Merion C.C. The drawing is by Everett Raymond Kinstler of New York City Grand Central Galleries.

Library of Congress Cataloging in Publication Data on File

ISBN 1-886947-02-3

Designed by I.Q. Press
Printed by The John Henry Company
Prepress by Grand AD Graphics & Design, Inc.

Printed in the United States of America
20 19 18 17 16 15 14 13 12 11 10 9 8 7 6 5 4 3 2

*Dedicated to Lauren, Geoffrey, and Skylar,
whose genuine familiarity with our Hero may
be as extensive and memorable as that of the author.*

*Bob Jones wore a shamrock on his watch chain
as he was born on St. Patrick's Day 1902.*

Table of Contents

Introduction

The life of Bobby Jones has been so publicly scrutinized and recorded in print and image that it is staggering indeed he and his family enjoyed any private moments at all. We thirst not only for glimpses which reveal the genuine ingredients contained in a singular champion, but also we yearn to witness the grace and humility with which greatness can be accommodated into our lives rather than serve as the catalyst of our destruction from unparalleled success. It is the earnest desire of your author that your wish be granted through the images contained in this volume. We must invoke the assistance of the SAGE in the discharge of such a daunting task.

Oh Sage, you have many challenging questions to be answered. What was our hero's upbringing as a youth, and what were the times and difficulties? How was his family knitted together and what of his family heritage? Show us the lean years which preceded the event never to be equalled in his sport. Now illuminate the Grand Slam in images never before seen and give us the context of the times. We want to see the adoring crowds and the unwatered fairways and the plus-fours and the hickory shafts on the rough greens. Let us glimpse our Hero traveling more miles, meeting more common and famous people, reading and writing more meaningful words, and exerting more positive influence as a role model than any politician, journalist, ambassador, or sportsman in memory.

Only pause briefly, Sage, and then satisfy our curiosity of our Hero's life after championship golf. What of the episodes in Hollywood making the stars themselves, stargazers? Take us fishing, hunting, camping, shooting, and recreating in the great outdoors. Endure the war for us and serve as our golf ambassador throughout the world. Conquer the people who would then love us by association through their love of our Hero. Let us see the bestowing of citizenship by a people who understand the difference between a ship which sits balanced in the water and one which "lists" toward talent without modesty and humility.

Take your canvas and paint for us a society which values a man who follows the rules, does what is right, and achieves the coveted title "gentleman." Make your brush sing with each stroke as you give depth of superb instincts and broad range of character. No matter what angle or what light is cast, make it sparkle with truth. Show us the price paid by our Hero for fame and genius of talent, richly appreciated and absorbed by the adoring crowds who are possessed of neither. Now, Sage, we are ready for the denouement in the gift of the ghost and dedication of a life through memorials of turf and treasured monument. Let this be accompanied by bands of angels who sing our sweet prince to his rest. As we end our pilgrimage over these pages, O Sage, let us glorify God in Heaven for the illumination of our lives through the wondrous deeds of our Hero. And, Sage, let there be laughter in our hearts and on our lips as we celebrate the vivid memory of our new-found Friend who has done all this for us.

Foreword

To many people, Bob Jones is a person who is larger than life. By the time he was 30, he had won all golf's major tournaments playing as an amateur, he had begun work on what would become the Augusta National Golf Club, he had earned two degrees (one in mechanical engineering and one in English literature),

and he had passed the Georgia Bar exam after being in law school for only one year. He also was married and the father of three children. To this day, his name is synonymous with the standards of the highest integrity.

Yet for all this, and for all that he did after age 30, his stature was the greatest in the eyes of a little boy who knew little about these accomplishments for which the world held him in

such awe. To this little boy, "Bub" was the greatest grandfather in the world, and his home was an adventure waiting to be explored. I was the little boy.

Every summer, my family would head south from our home in western Massachusetts to visit my maternal grandmother in south Georgia. On our way to her home, we would spend one week with my dad's parents, and we would spend another week with them on our way back to Massachusetts. Mr. and Mrs. Robert Tyre Jones, Jr. (Mary and Bob to their friends,

"Neenah" and "Bub" to their grandchildren), lived in an imposing white mansion off of Tuxedo Road in the Buckhead section of northwest Atlanta.

My grandparents always made me feel as though I were special. I would romp around the house, discovering the treasures that it held. Many of its treasures were found in the attic. There were boxes of Life magazines and old army uniforms with the silver oak leaves of a Lieutenant Colonel on the shoulders and an Army Air Corps patch on the sleeve. Also among this group were old radios and televisions, which I used *"to communicate with allied forces who had not yet invaded the European continent, as well as with friendly spacecraft who would help me save earth from Martian domination."*

There were treasures on the lower floors, as well. One object that particularly fascinated me was a globe which sat in the sun room. This globe was about 7 inches in diameter and it had four sterling-silver flags placed on it. The flags, two American and two British, were anchored in the globe at the approximate locations of the four sites of the Grand Slam tournaments. One day, while Neenah and Bub were upstairs with my parents, I decided that Bub deserved a special present and — with the thoughtfulness of a 4-year-old — I thought that the four silver flags would make a lovely gift.

With all the energy I could muster, I grabbed the first flag and gave it a yank. It came loose, but what followed was a 5-inch piece of wire which connected the flag to a post hidden in its center. Continuing with the focused attention of youth, I removed the three other flags and carried them up the stairs to give to my grandfather. I nervously walked in the room and held out my hands and told Bub that I had a present for him. My parents were apoplectic, and my grandmother was a shade of white which I had never seen before. Bub, however, looked at me and at my present and said, *"Son, that was so sweet of you to think of me. However, maybe in the future you could ask Neenah's permission before you bring me any more gifts."* I solemnly nodded my head and gave the flags to her.

Another treasure which I unearthed was Bub's record collection. He was a great lover of symphonic music and opera and had a decent collection of albums. My first discovery was his recording of Verdi's classic opera, *Rigoletto.* When Bub came home from work, he found me listening to this opera in the living room. Remembering my earlier transgression with the flags, I was nervous as to what his reaction would be. Hoyt (his butler/valet) stopped his wheelchair and Bub said, *"What do you think of that, Son?"* I told him I thought it was the best music I had ever heard. He smiled and said, *"Well, that's fine. A taste for opera is something you can develop for the rest of your life. Do you want the record?"*

"Yes, sir," I said.

"Well, it's yours," he replied.

Not being a person of great tact, I asked him if I could have another record which I had discovered. This record set was of the Nine Beethoven Symphonies by Toscanini and the NBC Orchestra. They were in a magnificent brown leather case with a bronze medallion bearing the likeness of the conductor. Bub thought for a moment and said, *"Have you listened much to these?"*

Again, I 'fessed up. *"Yes, sir."*

He paused and looked at me for a long time before he said, *"These are the most prized records in my collection, and — if you promise to take good care of them — you may have them."*

I have them to this day.

Bub was a man of great warmth and caring. When he spoke to me, he always gave me the feeling that what I was saying was the most important thing he had ever heard. When he was displeased, he would let me know in a way which communicated his feelings, but never in a way which robbed me of my dignity as a person. I remember few great conversations or words of wisdom, but I will always remember the twinkle in Bub's eye and the pleasure of being in his company.

I am excited and honored to write the foreword to this book. Mr. Matthew has done an outstanding job in taking the reader behind the scenes in Bub's life and showing who Robert Tyre Jones, Jr. was as a man. When the reader finishes this volume, he or she will be aware that while Bob Jones was not larger than life, he did know how to live it to its fullest.

- Robert Tyre Jones IV

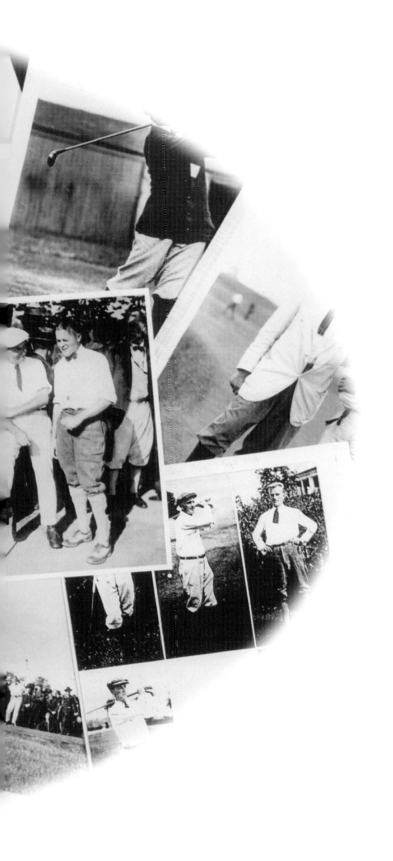

Chapter 1
Boy's Life

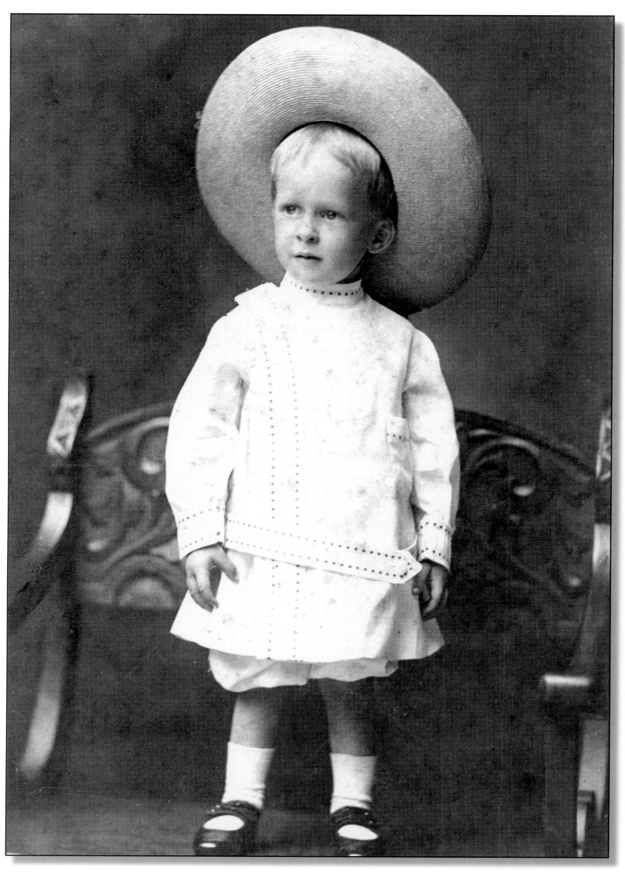

Robert Tyre Jones, Jr., was born on March 17, 1902, in the old L.P. Grant Homestead across from Grant Park in Atlanta. The family physician, Dr. Kendrick, delivered Bob in an old residence shared by his parents and their friends, Mr. and Mrs. Bryan M. Grant. A frail and sickly child, young "Rob" as he was called by his parents, was 5 years young before he could eat solid food.

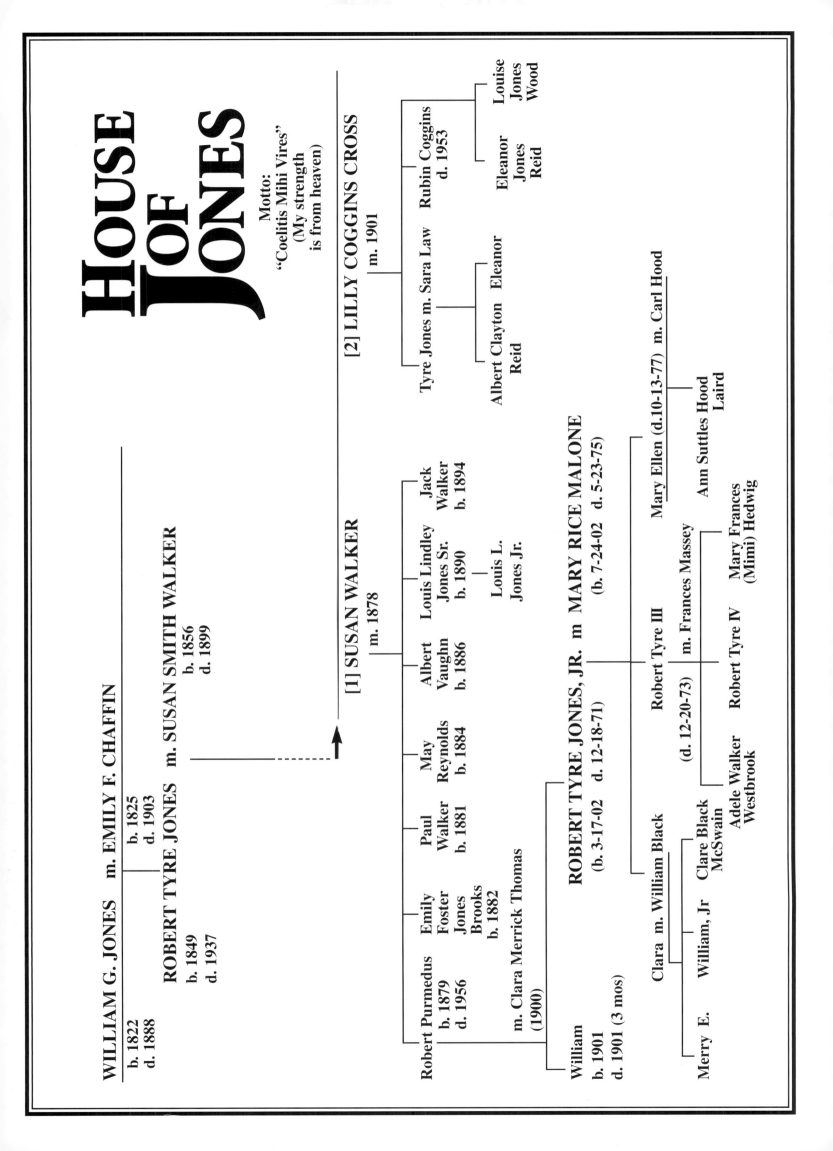

HOUSE OF JONES

Motto:
"Coelitis Mihi Vires"
(My strength
is from heaven)

WILLIAM G. JONES   m. EMILY F. CHAFFIN
b. 1822   b. 1825
d. 1888   d. 1903

ROBERT TYRE JONES   m. SUSAN SMITH WALKER
b. 1849   b. 1856
d. 1937   d. 1899

[1] SUSAN WALKER
m. 1878

Robert Purmedus
b. 1879
d. 1956
m. Clara Merrick Thomas
(1900)

William
b. 1901
d. 1901 (3 mos)

Emily
Foster
Jones
Brooks
b. 1882

Paul
Walker
b. 1881

May
Reynolds
b. 1884

Albert
Vaughn
b. 1886

Louis Lindley
Jones Sr.
b. 1890

Louis L.
Jones Jr.

Jack
Walker
b. 1894

[2] LILLY COGGINS CROSS
m. 1901

Tyre Jones m. Sara Law

Albert Clayton   Eleanor
Reid

Rubin Coggins
d. 1953

Eleanor
Jones
Reid

Louise
Jones
Wood

ROBERT TYRE JONES, JR. m MARY RICE MALONE
(b. 3-17-02   d. 12-18-71)   (b. 7-24-02 d. 5-23-75)

Clara m. William Black
(d. 12-20-73)

Robert Tyre III

Mary Ellen (d.10-13-77) m. Carl Hood

Merry E.

William, Jr

Clare Black
McSwain

Adele Walker
Westbrook

m. Frances Massey

Robert Tyre IV

Mary Frances
(Mimi) Hedwig

Ann Suttles Hood
Laird

Bob was named for his paternal grandfather, Robert Tyre Jones, (1849-1937), who stood 6 feet 5 inches tall and weighed 235 pounds. At age 30, "R.T." moved his family from the farm near Covington, Georgia, to Canton, where he established the Jones Mercantile Company in 1879. In 1899, R.T. started the Canton Cotton Mill, and by 1925 earnings exceeded $1.5 million. An upright moral man, R.T., told his grandson sternly, *"Bob, if you have to play golf on Sunday, play well."*

Bob's father was Robert Purmedus Jones (1879-1956). An Atlanta lawyer, the Colonel was an excellent athlete. (He was drafted by the "Brooklyn Superbas," later the Brooklyn Dodgers). He was gregarious, witty, humorously profane, and completely devoted to his wife, Clara, and son, "Rob."

A friend of the Jones family, Walter Brown, took this earliest known golfing picture of Bobby Jones when he was 6 years old at the East Lake course. Bob began to follow the best player at the club, professional Stewart Maiden, and imitate his swing. He never had any formal lessons.

O.B. Keeler wrote of this photo:

The cut portrays a scrubby, tousled-haired youngster, still with skinny arms and legs; just a typical American small boy about halfway through grade school. You could pick out dozens of boys at any recess period who looked a lot more like championship prospects at golf or any other sport, though it is unlikely that anyone of the dozens, or any boy of that age you could find in all the world, could swing a golf club as the youthful Bobby was swinging it then. The picture, however, indicates a somewhat flatter method than he employed later, when his style became an international concern as the "glass of fashion and mold of form." Still, it was a very good and sound little swing.

At the age of 11, Bobby shot an 80 on the old course at East Lake for the first time (par was 73). After his friend, Perry Adair, signed on the line marked "attested," Bob ran to the 14th green and solemnly handed the Colonel the card. His dad looked at the card, then Bobby, and with wet eyes hugged his son like no other. It was also in 1913 Bob first saw Harry Vardon and Ted Ray in an exhibition at East Lake.

In 1914, an Atlanta Journal reporter named Milt Saul told the editor, Major John S. Cohen, that he was playing in a tournament at the East Lake Club against a 12-year-old squirt named Little Bob Jones. *"They really ought not to allow these kids in the tournaments. Of course I'll beat him, but what's the good of taking up time beating children?"* Later, the Major asked how the match with Little Bob came out, and Saul confessed, *"He licked me 6-5! I still think I was right – they ought not to allow these kids in regular tournaments."*

The Druid Hills Club champion of 1915, Bob Jones (13 years old) defeated Archer Davidson while breaking the course record with a 73 and winning his first gold medal. Bob later lost the medal while playing Druid Hills in the same year and found it by the *"simple but laborious process of going with two caddies over every shot he had played in the round."* (The medal got away one other time-that time for good and was never found again.)

In June 1917, Bob became the youngest player ever to win the Southern Amateur (15 years, 3 months), which was played at Roebuck Springs Country Club in Birmingham, Alabama. That title was added to the Georgia State Amateur won in 1916 at the Capital City Country Club in Atlanta.

Chapter 2
The "Dixie Whiz Kid"

One lovely spring day in 1915, Grantland Rice stood with Alex Smith and Long Jim Barnes, both Open champions, watching 13-year old Bob Jones *"violently reposition"* his club after hitting a shot not to his liking. Smith disapproved of what he saw. *"It's a shame, but he'll never make a golfer...too much temper."* Barnes was more insightful. *"I disagree...this kid will be one of the world's greatest in a few more years."* Rice added: *"He isn't just satisfied with just a good shot. He wants it to be perfect — stone dead."* *"But you're correct about that temper, Alex. He's a fighting cock...a hot head. If he can't learn to control it, he'll never play the kind of golf he'll be capable of shooting."*

The youngest competitor in the U.S. Amateur championship of 1916, contested at the Merion Cricket Club, was a blue-eyed, towheaded 165-pound boy of 5 feet 4 inches tall named Bob Jones. He shot the lowest qualifying medal round, and that *"new kid from Dixie"* became an overnight sensation.

Sports **The Atlanta Journal.** Sports

VOL. XXXIV. NO. 164. H ATLANTA, GA., SUNDAY MORNING, AUGUST 6, 1916. PRICE FIVE CENTS

Rogers Fell Before Perry And Thrasher

Nashville's "No-Hit" King Is Outpitched by Atlanta's Bear-Cat and "Watkinsville Walloper" Finished Him With a Mighty Home Run

DOUBLE - HEADER DIVIDED

After Crackers Had Beaten Rogers in First Game the Vols Captured the Second Behind Air-Tight Pitching of Dick Wells

BY MORGAN BLAKE

THE great arm of Scott Perry and the mighty bat of Frank Thrasher proved too much for the illustrious Tom Rogers, pride of the Nashville hurling corps yesterday and the "No-Hit" King bit the dust in a gruelling pitching duel to the tune of 2 to 1. The Vols however came back and won the second contest of the double header by a similar score. The haughty league leaders left our midst last night and they were mighty glad to depart. They managed to win two games of the five and they were darn lucky to get them.

Both games yesterday were highly exciting and nip and tuck from first to last. To initial engagement early dedeveloped into a pitcher's battle between Perry and Rogers and Scotty far outshone his rival in the box. For six innings not a hit was made off the delivery of the Cracker bear-cat and when Atlanta made one run in the sixth it looked like Scotty had a shut out battle at least as the contest was only scheduled for seven innings. But Dick Kauffman singled to start the seventh, went to third on two infield outs and scored on Gabby Street's timely bingle to center.

This necessitated an extra inning and after Nashville had been retired in the eighth Frank Thrasher packed the game away. Two were out at the time and nobody on when big Frank stepped up to the plate. The fans had settled down for a long extra inning game when Rogers shot over a ball to liking of the Watkinsville walloper. Frank swung on it with all his force and lifted it over the right field sign. He trotted around the bases while the tremendous crowd in the grand stand and bleachers raised a mighty din. Frank got an ovation and also something a little more substantial in the nature of a fat purse from the audience.

IN this game Scott Perry continued the wonderful work in the box that he has given vent too in the past month. In the third inning he walked three men and filled the bases, but retired the side without a run. Up to the seventh, as stated above, not a hit was made by Nashville. Two hits in the seventh counted a run and two hits in the eighth threatened but did no damage.

Atlanta's first run came in when Yerkes singled and stole second and scored on Mayer's single to left. This was in the sixth inning.

In the second game the Crackers were helpless before Dick Wells, who held them to three hits and one run. This run was scored in the first inning when Tex McDonald led off with a triple over Lee's head and scored on Reilly's sacrifice fly to left.

Nashville's two runs came in the second when Kauffman singled and scored on Roy Ellam's long drive over Mayer's head for three bags. Roy tallied on Marshall's slashing single to left.

After this round, Ad Brennan pitched a game holding the Vols to one hit in the remaining five innings. But the damage had been done and with Wells pitching airtight ball the Crackers could not retrieve. In the second Mayer singled, went to third on Munch's hit to center and was caught at the plate when he and Munch tried a double steal. This was a mighty close play and to many it looked like Sammy had beat the throw. But Umps Morgan ruled different and his word was law.

FIRST GAME.

CRACKERS—	AB.	R.	H.	O.	A.	E.
McDonald, 3b.	4	0	2	0	3	1
Reilly, ss.	4	0	0	2	1	0
Moran, lf.	4	0	1	3	0	0
Thrasher, rf.	4	1	1	1	0	0
Yerkes, 2b.	3	1	2	3	6	0
Mayer, cf.	2	0	1	3	0	0
Munch, 1b.	3	0	0	11	0	0
Perkins, c.	3	0	0	1	0	0
Perry, p.	2	0	0	0	4	0
Totals	29	1	7	24	14	1

VOLS—	AB.	R.	H.	O.	A.	E.
Lee, cf.	3	0	0	0	0	0
Sheehan, 2b.	3	0	1	5	3	2
Baker, rf.	4	0	1	1	0	0
Williams, lf	4	0	0	2	0	0
Kauffman, 1b.	4	1	1	7	1	0
Kores, 3b.	2	0	0	1	2	0
Ellam, ss.	2	0	0	1	2	0
Street, c.	2	0	1	6	2	0
Rogers, p.	3	0	0	0	2	0
Totals	27	2	4	23	12	2

Score by innings—		R.	H.	E.
Atlanta	000 001 01—2		7	1
Nashville	000 000 10—1		4	2

Summary: Home run, Thrasher; sacrifice hits, Streeet, Mayer, Kores; struck out, by Rogers 2; bases on balls, Perry 3, Rogers 1; left on bases, Nashville 8, Atlanta 7. Umpires O'Toole and Morgan.

SECOND GAME.

ATLANTA.	AB.	R.	H.	PO.	A.	E.
McDonald, 3b	3	1	1	1	1	1
Reilly, ss.	1	0	0	2	1	0
Moran, lf	3	0	0	3	0	0
Thrasher, rf	3	0	0	0	0	0
Yerkes, 2b.	3	0	0	1	2	0
Mayer, cf	2	0	1	5	1	0
Munch, 1b	2	0	1	6	1	0
Perkins, c	2	0	0	3	1	0
Brennan, p	2	0	0	0	1	0
Totals	21	1	3	21	8	1

NASHVILLE.	AB.	R.	H.	PO.	A.	E.
Lee, cf	3	0	1	3	0	0
Sheehan, 2b	3	0	0	0	2	0
Baker, rf	3	0	0	0	0	0
Williams, lf	3	0	0	2	0	0
Kauffman, 1b	3	1	1	10	0	0
Kores, 3b	3	0	0	1	1	0
Ellam, ss	2	1	1	1	3	1
Marshall, c	2	0	2	4	2	0
Wells, p	2	0	0	0	0	0
Totals	24	2	5	21	8	1

Atlanta	100 000 0—1
Nashville	020 000 0—2

Summary: Three-base hits, McDonald, Ellam; sacrifice hits, Reilly; struck out, by Brennan 3, by Wells 4; left on bases, Nashville 5, Atlanta 3. Time of game, 1:25. Umpires, Morgan and Wilson.

Young Bob Jones Who Captured Final Match in State Golf Title Tournament

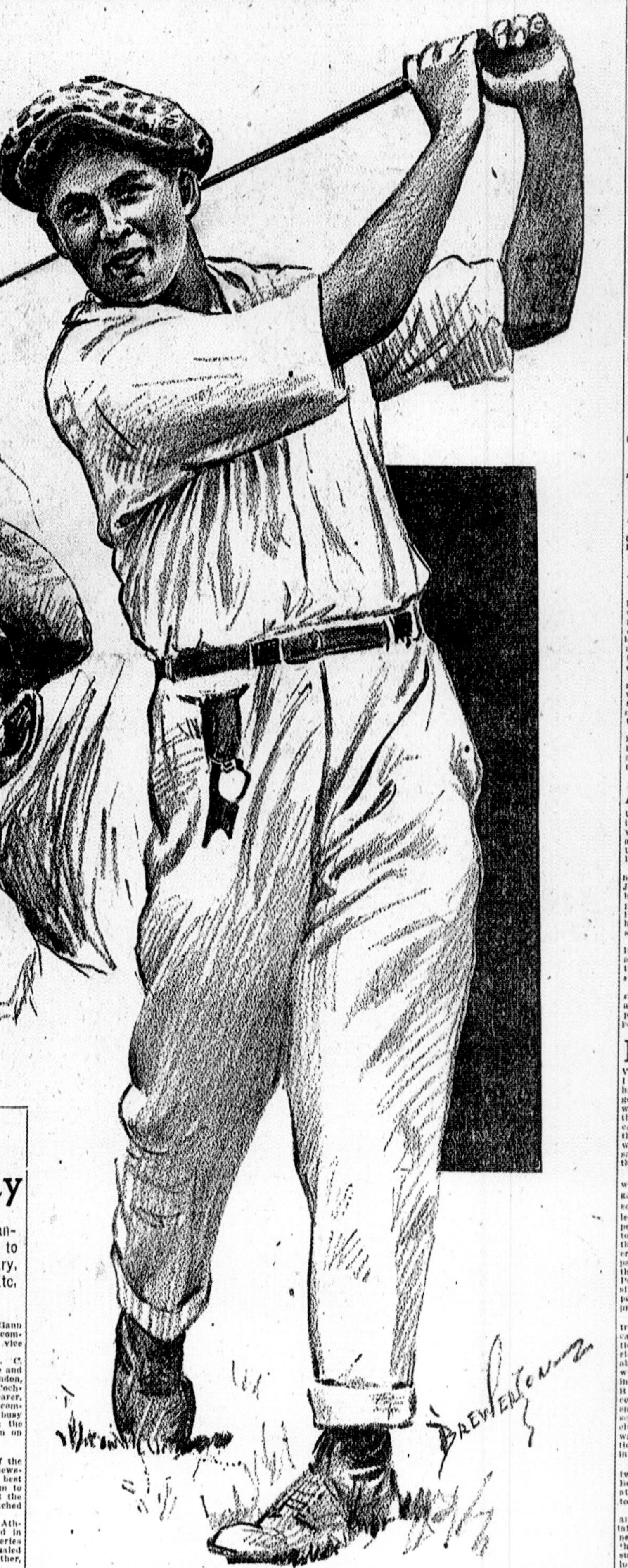

Playing the 36 holes at Brookhaven two strokes under par yesterday afternoon, Little Bob Jones not only won the state championship, but displayed a brand of golf that for sheer quality has never been equaled on a southern links. It is doubtful if ...

Great Sport Carnival Here on Labor Day

Held Under Auspices of Atlanta Federation of Labor—Randolph Rose Will Stage Big Boxing Contests, Bringing to Atlanta Some of the Most Prominent Pugilists in Country, Other Events Will Be Foot Races, Baseball Games, Etc. A Great Gala Day

ATLANTA'S greatest athletic carnival, the like of which has never been staged here before, is on the card for Labor day, starting in the afternoon and running into the night.

The affair is being staged under the auspices of the Labor day amusement committee of the Atlanta Federation of Trades, and according to present plans, will consist of athletic events of all kinds, including the best boxing matches obtainable, baseball games, foot races, band playing contests, and other events of interest.

The Labor day program is to be strictly a benefit affair. The cleanest and best of all sports will be staged, so as to make the affair long remembered by those who attend. The afternoon games will be held at the local park, while the boxing contests will be held in the evening at the city auditorium.

Due to the fact that Randolph Rose, the prominent sportsman and business man of Atlanta and Chattanooga, through his athletic club, the Randolph Rose A. B., in a business to get the leading boxers in the country, Mr. Rose will work with the committee in charge of the musements of that day in arranging the day and evening's entertainments.

At the meeting of the Atlanta Federation of Trades' amusement committee last Thursday President R. M. Gann placed Mr. Rose on the amusement committee, and he was at once elected vice chairman of this board.

Acting in conjunction with W. C. Puckett, chairman of the committee and a prominent boxing fan; W. L. Herndon, C. B. Reeves, W. L. Dorman, J. O. Cochran, Z. C. Cathright and J. M. Shearer, other members of the amusement committee, Mr. Rose will at once get busy in securing the leading boxers in the country to show at the auditorium on Labor day night.

Mr. Rose will also get the aid of the sporting editors on the three daily newspapers in arranging the very best matches. It will be Mr. Rose's aim to get the boys in the country, but at the same time have them as evenly matched as possible.

The work of the Randolph Rose Athletic club will be well remembered in Chattanooga. Mr. Rose staged a series of bouts there that were never equaled in that city, but, due to the hot weather, he decided to quit staging them.

The profits of the entire Labor day affair will go to the benefit of the Atlanta Federation of Trades. The boxing contests in the evening are sure to attract a very large crowd, and every

(Continued on Third Sport Page.)

Bob Jones Wins State Golfing Championsh

Plays Remarkably Fine G During Afternoon Sess and Takes Match 2 Up 36 Holes—Bob Played Final 18 in 70 Strokes, Better Than Par

GOLF ASSOCIATION FORM

Will Hold Tourneys Each Ye in Different Cities—Sava nah May Get the Event Ne Year—Dr. J. A. Selden, Macon, Elected Preside Lowry Arnold 1st Vice Pr

BY WARD GREENE

YOU reach the eighteenth hole Brookhaven with a long dr across the water hazard, a l brassie shot over the crest of the and a long iron to the green. It' long hole and a hard hole, and it a long fight and a hard fight that en on the eighteenth hole yesterday w Little Bob Jones won the first state championship from Perry Adair.

It was almost sunset when they c toiling over the last rise of the after a day of grueling combat in wh each youngster had played the best of his career. A tremendous gall was trailing them, hundreds of and women coatless and hatless horribly hot.

They had watched the two start on the last eighteen holes of their hole match with Perry three up on rival. They had seen Little Bob cut lead to two up at the turn. And t had watched him, playing like a mach that is hardly human, take hole a hole until he had squared the ma on Number eleven and put himself up on sixteen. They saw Perry t the next hole and now, at the last, w Little Bob only one up, it was the a test.

TWO long drives side by side do the center, two long brassies o the crest of the hill, and b boys took their irons. Little Bob's s was on the green, but a full fifteen f from the cup. Perry's was in the gra edge where he could use his putter. he could do the well-nigh impossil and hole out in one putt, he would squ the match and have a fighting cha on the nineteenth hole.

But it was too much to ask of a man, much less a nineteen-year-old b who for hours had been taxing ev nerve and muscle and now, in an most sickening silence, must stake eve thing on one little stroke.

His putt was two feet short of hole. Bob's putt almost rimmed tin. Perry took two more putts a a six. Bob sunk his for a five. A the match was over.

AS the youngsters shook hands in t center of the little plot of gre a patter of applause broke fr the crowd. And while they were che ing a champion, they were cheering well for the vanquished, and most all for an exhibition of skill and g that has not been duplicated on a Dix links since Scotland gave us the gam

As a finish to the first state tou nament ever held in Georgia, t Jones-Adair match left nothing be desired in the quality of the ga put up by the two title contenders the quantity of critical moments a hair-raising thrills that studded eve step of the way.

Both boys played the game of the lives. They drove hard and far. The approaches were perfect. On the gree they ran down putts apparently impo sible.

The figures on the last eighteen hole speak for themselves. Little Bob h a 70, Perry a 75. Bob went out par and came back two strokes unde par.

"I HAVE never seen such golf in m life," said a veteran player afte the match, "and I have watche Vardon, Evans and Travers at their be I don't believe any golfer living cou have beaten Bob Jones the way he wa going on that last eighteen holes. was wierd, something that went outsi the realms of human endeavor and b came supernatural. If I live to be thousand and die in poverty, I will a ways be proud that I can say, 'Well, saw Bob Jones and Perry Adair pla their famous match at Brookhaven.'"

The gallery that followed the mat will agree with him. It was the larges gallery that ever trailed a match in th south, and it was the best behaved ga lery. The spectators were so intereste personally in the players, so anxious no to breathe, a sound that would hinde the fraction of a stroke, that the re eree's "Fore" was hardly necessary t pause them at the proper place. Banke three deep around the greens as Bob o Perry leaned to his putt, they were s silent that the scratching of a newspa per man's pencil sounded like the ap proach of a cavalry charge.

And no wonder, for they were bein treated to an exhibition such as yo can't buy for the price of a seaso ticket to grand opera or the world's se ries—perfect golf, the kind you drea about after a duffer's day and the wil wish that you could reduce that scor into a semblance of respectability. Ye it was dream golf, played under perfec conditions—a hot blue sky overhead an snappy, springy turf underneath. Suc scores could have been made only at club like Brookhaven, where the fair ways are clear of treacherous obstruc tions and the whole course has been pu into first-class shape.

It was the second time this year th two boys have met in the finals, littl Bob winning the invitation tournamen at East Lake from Perry, 1 up and to play.

The match yesterday was far closer, and for a while Adair seemed a cer tain winner. It was Little Bob's steady nerve and sheer pluck in an uphill figh that won the last round for him an snatched back the prize when it seeme lost beyond all hope.

When they started out on that fina eighteen holes, Perry was three up The morning round had been his o nearly every hole, despite the dogge determination of Little Bob to over haul him. The latter seemed to be

In 1917, Bob played in numerous exhibition events for the benefit of the American Red Cross and the War Relief effort, raising over $150,000. Wealthy patrons paid $100 for the privilege of caddying for the amateur stars. Bob was encouraged in these endeavors by his mentor, Stewart Maiden (above and right).

During the 1917 exhibition matches, Bob was the only member of the amateur side who escaped a defeat against the professionals in the matches played at the Baltusrol Golf Club, Short Hills, New Jersey. Bob defeated Cyril Walker, 1 up. Walker would later win the U.S. Open in 1924.

The young Georgian began to gain inches and lose pounds in the three years following his debut at Merion. By 17, Bob was 5 feet 7 inches tall and weighed 150 pounds. He broke the course record shooting a 70 in a match played in Ft. Worth.

Bobby Jones and Chick Evans, who defeated Bob in the Western Amateur Championship of 1920 at Memphis. Bob never lost to the same man twice and exacted his revenge in the 1926 National Championship at Baltusrol, defeating Evans in the quarter finals, 3 and 2. In 1916, Evans made history, winning both the American Amateur and Open Championships.

In his early years, Bob always played against a definite personal opponent – playing against somebody, not against something. He had to learn *"that matching shots with the most debonair of human adversaries is at the best a feeble and uncertain pattern, compared with the iron certitudes of Old Man Par."*

During the Seven Lean Years, Bob told Keeler, *"I can play this game only one way. I must play every shot for all that is in it."* He later took to heart sage advice: *"The best shot, Bobby, is not always the one to play."*

Harry Vardon, the Old Master of Golf, and Bobby Jones, the Young Master, as they started their qualifying round together in Bobby's first National Open Championship, in 1920 at Toledo. Vardon predicted after that tournament that Jones would become one of the greatest golfers the game has known. Vardon missed winning the tournament by a single stroke, finishing in a tie with Leo Diegel, Jock Hutchison, and Jack Burke, a stroke back of Ted Ray, another great English professional.

By July 1921, at the age of 19 years and 4 months, Jones had competed in three U.S. Amateur Championships, one U.S. Open, one British Amateur, and one British Open. After the National Open played at the Columbia Country Club at Washington, Walter Hagen told O.B. Keeler:

Bobby was playing some great golf, in spots. He's got everything he needs to win any championship except experience, and maybe philosophy. He's still a bit impetuous. But I'll tip you off to something — Bobby will win the Open before he wins the Amateur!

In September 1921, Jones and Keeler went by train to St. Louis for the National Amateur Championship. Bobby said, *"I wonder if I'm ever going to win one of these things."* Keeler replied, *"Bobby, if you ever get it through your head that whenever you step out on the first tee of any competition, you are the best golfer in it, then you'll win this championship and a lot of others."*

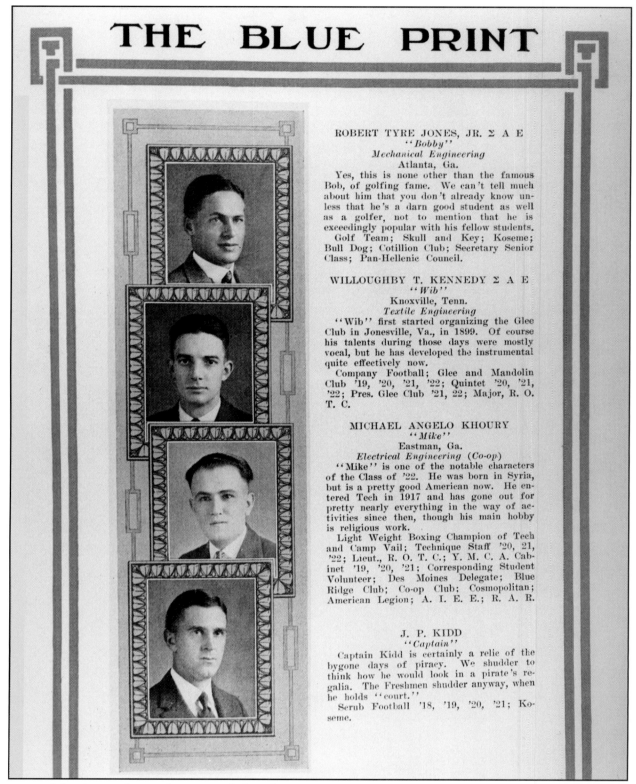

THE BLUE PRINT

ROBERT TYRE JONES, JR. Σ A E
"Bobby"
Mechanical Engineering
Atlanta, Ga.

Yes, this is none other than the famous Bob, of golfing fame. We can't tell much about him that you don't already know unless that he's a darn good student as well as a golfer, not to mention that he is exceedingly popular with his fellow students.

Golf Team; Skull and Key; Koseme; Bull Dog; Cotillion Club; Secretary Senior Class; Pan-Hellenic Council.

WILLOUGHBY T. KENNEDY Σ A E
"Wib"
Knoxville, Tenn.
Textile Engineering

"Wib" first started organizing the Glee Club in Jonesville, Va., in 1899. Of course his talents during those days were mostly vocal, but he has developed the instrumental quite effectively now.

Company Football; Glee and Mandolin Club '19, '20, '21, '22; Quintet '20, '21, '22; Pres. Glee Club '21, 22; Major, R. O. T. C.

MICHAEL ANGELO KHOURY
"Mike"
Eastman, Ga.
Electrical Engineering (Co-op)

"Mike" is one of the notable characters of the Class of '22. He was born in Syria, but is a pretty good American now. He entered Tech in 1917 and has gone out for pretty nearly everything in the way of activities since then, though his main hobby is religious work.

Light Weight Boxing Champion of Tech and Camp Vail; Technique Staff '20, 21, '22; Lieut., R. O. T. C.; Y. M. C. A. Cabinet '19, '20, '21; Corresponding Student Volunteer; Des Moines Delegate; Blue Ridge Club; Co-op Club; Cosmopolitan; American Legion; A. I. E. E.; R. A. R.

J. P. KIDD
"Captain"

Captain Kidd is certainly a relic of the bygone days of piracy. We shudder to think how he would look in a pirate's regalia. The Freshmen shudder anyway, when he holds "court."

Scrub Football '18, '19, '20, '21; Koseme.

Bob's Georgia Tech annual for the year 1922. Georgia Tech Dean Emeritus George C. Griffin remembered: *"Bob was a good student, never in trouble, who was popular with his classmates, a class officer and active in all school activities. He was a real gentleman in every respect, modest, unassuming, never mentioning his golf game. All in all, a real all-around young American. He was honest as the days are long and had a kind heart, willing for everyone to have their worldly goods. He also had a great sense of humor."*

Bob graduated from Tech High School in Atlanta at the age of 16. He received a degree in mechanical engineering from Georgia Tech at age 20 (1922). He entered Harvard and received a B.S. in English literature in 1924. In 1926-27, Bob attended one year of Emory University Law School and took the bar exam to see how difficult it would be. To his amazement, he passed it and was admitted to the Georgia Bar in 1928, joining his father's law firm.

Bobby Jones and George Duncan, the brilliant English professional, played the last two rounds together at Skokie (Chicago) in the 1922 U.S. Open Championship in which Bobby finished a single stroke behind Gene Sarazen. Duncan had previously won the British Open Championship in 1920 at Deal, England.

During his first year at Harvard University, Bob practiced for the 1923 U.S. Open. He had already exhausted his eligibility playing undergraduate golf at Georgia Tech. Bob got his crimson "H" by assuming the position of assistant team manager. Jones single handedly defeated all six of the top Harvard golfers pooled together in an informal match and became a member of the Harvard Varsity Hall of Fame even though he never formally competed. Two months after this photo was taken, Jones won his first major championship at Inwood.

Gene Sarazen and Bob Jones talking it over at the Inwood Country Club in 1923. After Sarazen won the 1922 U.S. Open, he never defeated Jones in any Open Championship, British or American, from 1923-1930. Sarazen wrote of Jones, *"Bob was a fine man to be partnered with in a tournament...He made you feel that you were playing with a friend, and you were."*

At Inwood, Bob's play from the sand with a niblick was extraordinarily good. Others, including Hagen, couldn't "blast" the ball and suffered using a "chipping" technique from the bunker.

The Atlanta youth was in a dejected frame of mind when he finished his final round even before Cruickshank forced a playoff with a final birdie. Jones refused to accept the premature congratulations of his admirers:

I don't want to win the title this way. I know what they're saying. They think I'm a quitter because I had the championship in my pocket and chucked it away. And they're right. I fell down shamefully when all I had to do was chip over that little trap.

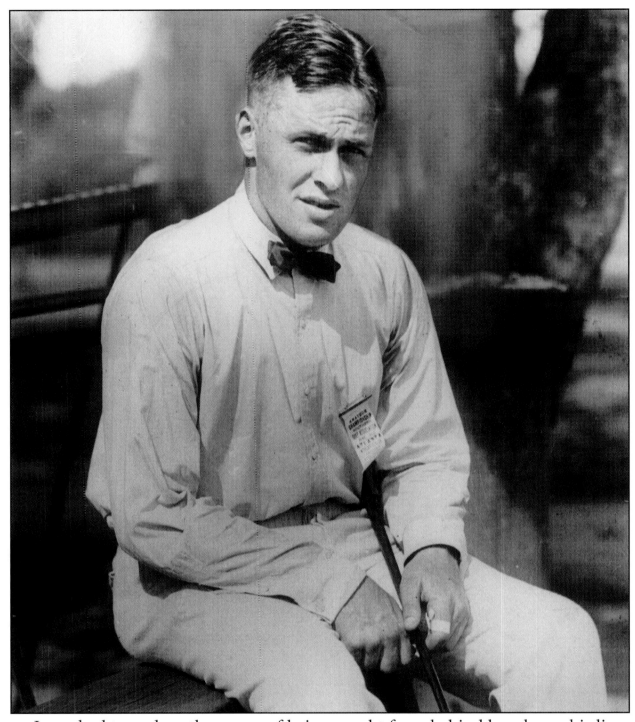

Jones had to endure the agony of being caught from behind by a brave birdie negotiated on the last hole by wee Bobby Cruickshank. In a letter to O.B. Keeler, Cruickshank wrote:

The greatest shot I ever made in my life was that iron shot at the 18th hole at Inwood to tie Bobby Jones as I stood on the 18th tee and looked down that treacherous stretch of course and on to the still more treacherous water guarding the green. My thoughts were very mixed...My heart missed a few beats I know, but I took plenty of time to steady myself...The ball dropped ten yards short of the pin and trickled up 7 feet from the hole and I knew that my chance lay before me as things went I took it and made my birdie three.

Cruickshank and Jones prepare to playoff for the 1923 Open Championship.

Bobby Jones and Bobby Cruickshank join Stewart Maiden, Bobby Jones' mentor (on the extreme right), and Jimmy Maiden, Stewart's brother (on the extreme left).

On the last hole of the playoff, Jones gambled with a courageous shot over the lagoon guarding the front of the green and landed his ball seven feet from the hole for victory. Here Bob accepts the congratulations of Grantland Rice (right).

Winning of the United States Open Golf Championship

BOBBY JONES AT THE 18TH HOLE ON THE INWOOD LINKS, LONG ISLAND, IN THE GAME WHICH DECIDED IN HIS FAVOR THE CHAMPIONSHIP. ROBERT CRUIKSHANK, HIS OPPONENT, WHO HAD PREVIOUSLY TIED HIM, WAS THE RUNNER-UP. A GALLERY OF OVER 3,000 PEOPLE WITNESSED WHAT WAS A REMARKABLE EXHIBITION OF GOLF BY BOTH PLAYERS.

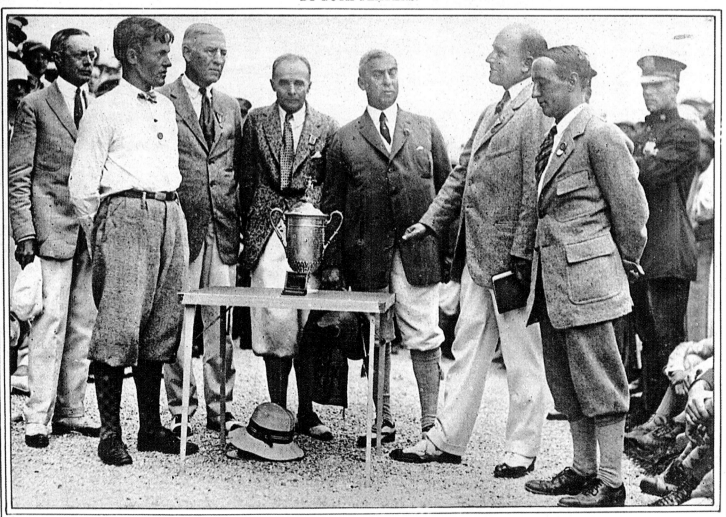

PRESENTATION TO BOBBY JONES, THE YOUNG GOLF WIZARD OF ATLANTA, GA., OF THE TOURNAMENT TROPHY WHICH WENT WITH HIS VICTORY FOR THE OPEN GOLF CHAMPIONSHIP. AT RIGHT FOREGROUND IS ROBERT CRUIKSHANK, WHO GAVE HIM SUCH A CLOSE RACE FOR THE TITLE.

The end of the Seven Lean Years for Bobby Jones, who has just won his first major title in the National Open of 1923 at Inwood. Tommy Logan, veteran sportsman, is just over Jones' right shoulder.

The 1923 U.S. Open champion greeted warmly by his fellow Atlantans.

Chapter 3
The Family Jones

Bob married childhood sweetheart Mary Rice Malone on June 17, 1924, in Atlanta.

The Family Jones. From left to right: Robert Tyre Jones III, Clara Malone Jones, and Mary Ellen in the arms of mother Mary.

Robert Tyre Jones III takes a lesson with Calamity Jane from his distinguished father. The young Jones, age 14, proudly returned a 95 in a one-day high school event. Father Jones was pleased his son played golf only for fun and not for money. The younger Jones went on to win the Atlanta City Championship and played against Jack Nicklaus in the first round of the 1959 U.S. Amateur Championship at the Broadmoor CC in Colorado Springs, Colorado.

"Two Bobs." Robert Tyre Jones, Jr., and Robert Tyre Jones III, who operated a Pittsfield, Massachusetts, Coca-Cola bottling plant owned by his father. Jack Nicklaus remembered the day he once played against Bob Jones' son:

In the 1959 Amateur, at Broadmoor, through the accident of the draw I came up against his son, Robert T. Jones III, in the first round. Young Bob is a very good player who has qualified for the Amateur quite a few times, and on his day he can give any golfer all that he can handle. That morning at Broadmoor, when young Bob and I met on the first tee, he greeted me with a big, warm smile. 'You might be interested in knowing, Jack,' he said, 'that my father was thinking of coming out for this tournament. Then when he found out who I had drawn as my first opponent, he changed his mind. He decided it wasn't worth a trip to Colorado just to watch me play one round.

Col. Robert P. Jones and his famous son at the opening of the Augusta National Golf Club in 1933. A happier and more warming relationship did not exist between father and son than between Bob and the Colonel. The Colonel

...likes to sing bass in the shower room; he likes people; he cusses in a manner that is musical and artistic and not at all offensive. He can question a man's ancestry and make it feel like a caress. He can create loyalty and devotion....They've got most of us in a mold — a few they can't get in. A few remain out. They are the men with real personality. They are the men whom people love and follow. The Colonel is one of those....He is a part of the soul of East Lake Club; one of the personalities who kept us going as something more than just brick and stone and lake and green and fairway.

"Three Bobs." Robert Tyre Jones, Jr.; Robert Tyre Jones IV; and Robert Tyre Jones III.

The spotlight of public attention focused upon the Jones family from it's earliest beginnings.

Clara and Bob III examine some of their father's memorabilia.

Chapter 4
Bobby Jones' Secret Weapon
O.B. Keeler

During his 16-year career in championship golf, Bob Jones carried in his arsenal what he called a "secret weapon." It was more potent than Calamity Jane, Jeanie Deans, or even his steel-trap concentration. Bob used his secret weapon in each one of his 13 major championship victories and even during the accomplishment of the Grand Slam in the Great Year of 1930. Bob's competitors respected and feared his secret weapon, and each of them likely wished they also had one just like Bob's. Bob could rely on his faithful secret weapon in the bad times and good. Bob's secret weapon traveled with him over 150,000 miles and never once let him down. Of course, the secret weapon was Oscar Bane Keeler.

From the time that O. B. ("Pop") Keeler began reporting on Bob Jones' golfing exploits in 1916, both fate and destiny forged these two together stronger than did any Scotch blacksmith a smooth-faced cleek make.

Their matchup was perfect because Keeler was as brilliant in his element as Jones proved to be in his. Keeler knew as much about golf as any sportswriter ever did - and he knew how to write about it. Pettersen Marzoni laid the following prose on the subject:

Let him who will dispute old Bill Keeler's part in Bobby's game. The writer doubts that the world's greatest champion will do so. Keeler knows more theoretical golf, perhaps, than any man living. He knows what makes every shot, though he can't make them. He knows what shot should be made and when. He has watched Bobby through the years until he can see a deviation from flawlessness that no other eye could catch.

H. G. Salsinger of the Detroit News also got it right when he observed:

Bobby Jones is the prince of golf but O. B. Keeler is his prophet and in adulation of the prince, the prophet has too often been neglected.

Jones would probably have become the prince of golf without the prophet but the royal purple of his robe would have lacked much of its illustrious sheen.

While Jones composed his epics, Keeler sang them to the world and they seemed all the finer for the manner of singing.

Here for more than a decade has been one of the finest combinations in all sport.

Pop was the only one who really knew the "book" on Bob Jones. Only he could call him "Rubber Tyre" to his face in jest and have him laugh openly because of the deep roots of affection common to both. Only Pop knew details such as Bob having made two holes in one: the first at No. 11 (175 yards) at the East Lake C.C. and No. 14 at Augusta C.C. Keeler served not only as Bob's publicist and historian, but he also filled those duties for the entire Fourth Estate for which Pop was equally loved, respected, and admired. Fellow reporters deemed it honor enough just to carry his typewriter. It was Keeler who first penned the lines that were often and accurately repeated by Jones to such an extent they became his own:

BOBBY JONES' SECRET WEAPON — O. B. KEELER

Golf is the closest game to the game we call life. You get bad breaks from good shots; you get good breaks from bad shots — but you have to play the game where it lies.

For his efforts, the Associated Press "anointed" O. B. as an honorary member in 1926. Keeler had obtained and shared with fellow reporters the first and only interview given by Jones at that time. Ed Sullivan wrote in his newspaper column "Sport Whirl" of Keeler's help given to other reporters:

Undoubtedly O. B. Keeler helped groove Bobby's character just as his swing was grooved by the great instructor of Alexa Stirling.

The transition from the club-breaking Jones to the record-breaking Jones, the change from the fiery, impatient Jones to the subdued Jones — this must be traced in large measure to the influence of Keeler.

In the passage of years the older man and the younger never grated on each other's nerves. Keeler might explain that by pointing out that he never intruded on Bobby's private life.

If O. B.'s close contacts with Bobby were advantageous they also served as a definite handicap. Wires of congratulations from all over the country rewarded me for telling exclusively of Jones' moving picture contract, but Keeler, not I, had the story first.

Yet Keeler, because he was on intimate terms with Bobby, was compelled in honor to withhold the story that stirred both continents and aroused echoes in the British Parliament.

Certainly he had the story first. He was Bobby's confidant and he was his adviser.

Keeler never begrudged his information. Whenever I went out to cover a golf tourney I'd always ring O. B. just as soon as I got into town. He could always scrape up a readable yarn for an impoverished writer and he did it so cheerfully that you always left him with the feeling that you had done him a favor in tapping his mine of information.

Jones has been honored, time and again, for what he did for the Southland, but although a Northerner hesitates to suggest matters of policy to the South, I suggest in all earnestness that the Atlanta Chamber of Commerce convene and strike off a medal to O. B. Keeler for his services.

In 1949 Atlanta did organize a testimonial dinner for Keeler. More than 300 friends assembled at Druid Hills Golf Club to celebrate 40 years of newspaper work. By that time Pop had covered 67 major golf tournaments in the United States and Great Britain. The invitation read "Strictly Stag" prompting a tongue-in-cheek "demand" by Clifford Roberts for an "interpretation." It was not necessary to use high-pressure tactics in "selling" the $15 tickets since all of the attendees were unanimous in their conviction that Pop deserved the tribute. And ironically, most were 100-plus shooters on the course. The guest list was a "Who's Who" in media and sport, and they presented Keeler with a new Buick automobile.

Ralph Trost of the Brooklyn Eagle wired his regrets coupled with these accolades:

O. B. was a top man when I saw my first national championship. I rode on the Jones gravy train, so to speak, for I came into golf writing the year Bobby won his first. Inwood was my initiation. It was also my introduction to O. B.

For a great many more than one of us just breaking in, Keeler made Jones. He WAS Jones. He told us what Jones said, what he hoped, his aims. He told us what he had done — and much about what he was going to do, and did. Far more than Bob Jones can ever realize, many of us got to know Bobby through O. B.

There was around here some antagonism to Bob which he knew. O. B. finally killed it. The reason for it was more the golf officials than Bob. He was too closely guarded. I think, if Bob will recall, the "opposition" cracked after Baltusrol in '26. O. B., trekking in and out of the private quarters arranged for Bobby brought back the news to the first "Black Hole of Calcutta." There was one statement: Bobby said, "I just can't go on beating Von Elm every time, he's too good a player." None of us heard it, or probably would have heard it, but for O. B. it was very humane, very likeable coming from the man who was killing off all competition. I know I, for one, liked this humanness from the boy being pictured as a golf machine.

Ed Danforth of the Atlanta Journal echoed this tribute to Pop:

This Keeler had a vast store of golf lore and he shared it generously along the way to later comers into the field. He gave the world through personal contact and through the columns of the Atlanta Journal a colorful, honest, picture of Jones that otherwise never would have been possible, for Jones was modest and retiring and never thrived on the crowd.

Pop Keeler knew first hand the genuine truth of Bob's modesty:

It is our custom to travel and room together. Bobby is excessively retiring and even bashful and is embarrassed by strangers staring at him, and acquaintances, or perhaps strangers, coming up and talking with him. For this reason we always eat in the drawing room of the Pullman, if we have one, and in the room at the hotel or club. This is not at all an upstage business. Bobby simply dislikes the limelight and is annoyed by it.

We talk some about golf and the tournament at hand, but more about other matters. We always talk about his game impersonally. Bobby and his game are two different entities in the mind of each of us, and we can praise or pan it with equal impartiality. We try to study his game in perfect detachment. Bobby does not talk a great deal about golf when in a tournament, or about the tournament.

Bob more than tipped his hat to Pop in his remarks given on the occasion of the conferral of honorary A.P. membership upon Pop:

O.B. and I have been knocking around the world together for a long time. Our only rivals in actual mileage are the Roosevelt brothers, and they didn't catch up with us until they took that recent trip to Tibet.

O.B. is the greatest golf writer who ever lived. Golf is a game of psychology. It is played in the head. Grantland Rice and other golf writers are able to follow players around and see every stroke, describing a match play by play. But no other writer has the knowledge of the psychology of the game that O.B. Keeler has. There is no question about that, either in the minds of the golfers who take part in national play, or the writers who cover such tournaments. This is proven by the way the other writers hover around O.B. at all the big tournaments, to find out what O.B. is going to write, so they can do likewise.

This boy is the finest fellow and the greatest golf writer who ever lived, and he is about two years younger than I am. (Laughter)

Keeler could, therefore, be considered as the first "sports psychologist" or at least forerunner in a field that today employs professionals whose entire careers focus on that single area. If confidence is a necessary ingredient to a champion's success, perhaps Bob's psychologist provided a boost in 1921 when Bob turned dejectedly to Pop and said, *"I wonder if I will ever win a championship?"* Pop boldly replied, *"Son, you're the greatest golfer in the world and when you get that conviction in your skull, you'll win not one but a lot of them."*

Keeler "saw" all of Bob's 13 major titles, but ironically did not see the two most crucial shots that won Bob his medals. In 1929 Pop couldn't bear to watch the 12-foot putt against Espinosa at Winged Foot. He asked Al Watrous to later describe it for him. Watrous told Pop how to report the stroke:

The most perfectly gauged putt I ever saw. If that hole had been a 4-1/4 inch circle on the green, the ball would have stopped in the middle of it.

In 1926, at the British Open played at Royal Lytham and St. Annes, Bob was even with Al Watrous coming to the 17th hole. Jones' second shot from a *"sandy lie in broken ground"* was so perfectly struck that *"a teaspoon too much of sand could have ruined the shot."* Watrous was staggered enough by the shot to require three putts and give Bob the edge he needed to clinch victory.

Pop "confessed":

I did NOT see that shot. I followed that last round through the thirteenth hole where Bobby was still two strokes behind Watrous then I switched over to the clubhouse hoping against hope that if I quit watching the luck would change...It did. It did. I was over at the clubhouse in the bar taking on a liberal belt of antifreeze when the news came in.

Jones again generously acknowledged Pop's contributions to his successes at the testimonial dinner given Pop in 1949:

When the other players read how wonderful we were as described by O. B. a lot of the fight was taken out of them before they stepped on the first tee. And we were so filled with gratitude by the same dispatches that we had to go ahead and win for fear of letting O. B. down.

*   *   *

I've often thought about all the suffering I caused poor old Keeler. How he almost literally held my hand through the critical moments of my career. I thought he might need someone to hold his hand tonight and I am glad to be here to do it.

Bob later prepared a preface to "The Bobby Jones Story" by O. B. Keeler and Grantland Rice in which he explained:

O.B. Keeler and I enjoyed a very real partnership for the better part of twenty years. We traveled thousands of miles together, we lived our golf tournaments together, we wrote a book, did a radio series, and two motion pictures series, all in the closest and most harmonious collaboration. I doubt if ever such a relationship existed between performer and reporter in sport or elsewhere.

The ebb and flow of a player's confidence is one of the strange phenomena of competitive golf. I have discussed this angle with all the great players of my own and later eras and none deny or can explain the periods of uncertainty that occasionally come in the midst of the most complete assurance.

In the first qualifying round for the Amateur Championship at Minikahda in 1927 I posted a 75. I never wanted to win qualifying medals--a sort of superstition I suppose—and I had tried to coast along and do a modest, comfortable score. But I had slipped a stroke here and there and perhaps had been lucky to score 75. Suddenly I began to see that another slack round with a stroke or two more gone might leave me out of the tournament.

So I set out to find Keeler.

"O.B.," I said, "the only way for me to get out of this thing is to go out this afternoon and try to win the medal and I need you to walk with me for a few holes until I get calmed down."

I wanted just the satisfaction of having an understanding soul with me to get over that feeling of aloneness which comes when your confidence is gone. It worked like a charm. I let O.B. go after the fifth hole, finished the round in 67 for a course record and the medal, and went on to win the championship.

This is just one of the things I owe to Keeler. The bigger thing no one knows better than I or than the boys who were writing sports in those days. To gain any sort of fame it isn't enough to do the job. There must be someone to spread the news. If fame can be said to attach to one because of his proficiency in the inconsequential performance of striking a golf ball, what measure of it I have enjoyed has been due in large part to Keeler and his gifted typewriter.

I am asked now to say that I am willing to leave the record of my golfing activities to the words this man has written. Why in Heaven's name shouldn't I be? He never once gave me anything but the best of any argument.

At a 1955 anniversary party for Bob and The Grand Slam, Keeler's absence was conspicuous as Bob modestly declined to accept the entire mantle of greatness extended to him by his friends. Instead, Bob partly deferred to O. B.:

Keeler attributed so many fine qualities to me when we were traveling together that ultimately I began to take on some just from the suggestion. At least I hope I have.

Keeler's genius for writing stemmed partly from his gift of storytelling. Pop had a "tarbucket" mind and everything that went into it stuck. He had a seemingly endless reservoir of prose, poetry, and risque limericks. His eclectic interests ranged from opera to zebra racing to murder trials to gambling to classic literature to all sports.

Pop made four trips to the Rose Bowl covering football for Alabama, Auburn, and Georgia. He was also a competitive rifle shooter. Pop loved baseball too:

Baseball is the greatest of all spectator games. It is right out there where everyone can see what is going on.

In his youth, Pop was a first-class boxer, too, and he followed the sport closely enough to be photographed with heavyweight champion Primo Carnera. It was golf reporting, however, which placed him into a class by himself.

His skills were admired on both sides of the Atlantic. Bernard Darwin, the dean of British writers, confirmed such to be the case:

Incidentally, it was at the Walker Cup that I first met O. B. Keeler. He and I were fellow passengers after the match in a steam yacht from Southampton to New London. I was crushed by him in a quoting match and became, I hope, a friend of his from that day. He was a delightful person and, as readers will realize, an admirable writer, both sensitive and exciting. He was never afraid to let himself go, an essential quality in good writing on sport, and his devotion to his friend and patriotic adoration of Atlanta stand out on every page.

Pop developed a simple philosophy about writing newspaper stories:

When you sit down to write a story make believe you are writing a letter to a friend. Go ahead and address it "Dear Joe" and then tell your friend the news. Sign it in the customary way, if you please.

Then when you have finished, merely cross out the salutation and the "Yours Truly" and you have a news story.

Keeler admonished writers to establish a name for yourself and then always write up to it. *Don't ever let your by-line down."* In writing over a million words and more than 500 stories for Associated Press alone, Pop was emphatic that proper descriptive language be used in stories. One sure method to evoke an eruption of disgust and contempt was for a reporter to describe a golfer as *"burning up the course"* or *"racing around the course"* or *"galloping o'er the fairways"* or *"parading to the green."* Keeler would usually react by screaming out loud that golf is not a track meet coupled with colorful language that would never survive scrutiny of the other editors of the family newspaper. Whenever he was in position, Keeler took pleasure in first chiding the reporter for his faux pas and then editing the dickens out of the story of the golfer who was seen *"roaring home in under par."* In later years, when the new crop of writers kept violating the rule of descriptive precision honored by their predecessors like Pop, it was his wordsmithy that was sorely missed by the minority who knew the difference. Pop managed his pen with literary precision more likened to a rapier than a broadsword. He wrote word images which would endure:

It was an ideal day for football — too cold for the players and too cold for the spectators."

There are things in golf finer than winning championships.

and

This victory, the fourth major title in the same season and in the space of four months, has now and for all time entrenched Bobby Jones safely within the "Impregnable Quadrilateral of Golf," that granite fortress that he alone could take by escalade and that others may attack in vain forever.

Pop did not feel that profanity necessarily added to good literature. When fellow Atlanta writer Morgan Blake decried the necessity to paint a villainous character with profane filth, Pop wrote him a letter in wholehearted agreement:

Reading that column of yours about the current foulness, filth and profanity in so-called literature I'd like to suggest in contrast another book by R. L. Stevenson in "Treasure Island" written about the roughest characters in the world of that era, the English Pirates. And not one single oath in the book!

Pop spontaneously recalled that Long John Silver's spectacular flaming temper was aroused when he "spat in the spring" and then growled:

That's what I think of you! Them's as dies will be the lucky ones!

Keeler recited several pages verbatim from memory to support his thesis that no greater chills could have been summoned up his spine by having Silver snarl, *"You so and so and blankety, blank, blank."* (expletives deleted).

During World War II Keeler chided some of the American airmen and reporters who gleefully described the results of bombing raids as *"something beautiful to look upon."* Pop eloquently urged to omit the adjective "beautiful" when reporting on war and its ugly blight upon mankind. Pierce Harris wrote that this was the only remaining lit candle in an otherwise dreary time.

Pop was not only a prolific writer, but he was also accurate even to his typing. He regularly produced 10 pages of copy per hour without more than a single error, or perhaps two. He credited his typing accuracy to a prior job which required production of letter-perfect timetables for a Nashville Railroad company. No strikeovers or errors were allowed.

Once, before the days of Ed Danforth and Furman Bisher, O. B. took Morgan Blake aside and then called a group of other young writers accompanied by Bill Kinney and said:

Morgan did you write that with a pencil and correct it on the typewriter or did you write it on the typewriter and correct it with a pencil?

A "tarbucket" mind of elephantine proportions can be helpful to a reporter, as, for example, when Pop attended a famous trial in the Atlanta courts. When the judge read the verdict from the bench, there was no court reporter to record the proceedings by stenography or shorthand. Reporters rushed out of the courtroom to post their stories. Somehow, the judge discovered later that day he had lost the original verdict. The situation was easily remedied by the judge ordering the court stenographer to fetch a copy of Keeler's published copy of the verdict in the newspaper and to reproduce it verbatim as the official court version! After Keeler's report had been made "official," the judge found his lost original the very next day while rummaging through the papers on his desk. When the judge compared the original copy to Keeler's published newspaper report, the two were determined to be identical even to the punctuation marks.

Keeler was born in Chicago on Rush Street on June 4, 1882. He liked to say he was the *"first white child born in Chicago."* He was removed *"without his knowledge or consent"* at age 4 to Tate, Pickens County, Georgia, where his father was general manager of the Georgia Marble Company. O. B. attended Marietta High School where he devoted at least four years in the study of Latin and Greek, which would serve as a lifelong classical education foundation. The school was known later as the Waterman Street School, and Keeler etched not only his own name, but also his classmates names in the front-room windows. Until 1975 they were still visible. He graduated in 1898.

The first job O. B. took was in a bank. It was the beginning of a handful of business positions that did not agree with a man of classical training and of letters. Pop wrote the following "auto-obituary" (never published) and therein described the way he humorously viewed his career:

Ten and a half years after graduation Pop labored in (1) a bank, (2) a railroad office, (3) as treasurer of an iron foundry and machine works, (4) in the office of a marble finishing mill, (5) again in a railroad office, (6) in the office of a fertilizer manufacturing company and (7) coincidentally in the promotion of a silver mine in the Parral District of Old Mexico (he still has 15,200 shares of stock in it), and, losing this last job through insubordination -- he had offered to wager the boss $500 cash money that he (the Boss) could not name the team which would outfinish the Cubs in the National League in 1908 — finally in (8) the office of a fire insurance agency in which he was cashier and invented a system of bookkeeping which never has been of any use since, as no one who succeeded him could operate it.

At this stage, being then 26 1/2 years of age, with a wife and two small children, our hero decided to go out to the Chattahoochee River and drown himself, being distinctly discouraged with office work as a means of livelihood. His ambition always had been to work for a newspaper, but the various tentative and timorous approaches made by him had been coldly rebuffed on the reasonable ground that he had no previous experience. Being now desperate he made the offer, to The Atlanta Georgian, in December, 1908, that he would come over and work for The Georgian at nothing per week until such time as The Georgian could decide if he were worth more, or less.

Not seeing any good way of losing on the deal, The Georgian took up this proposition, over the protest of its then managing editor, Mr. Milt Saul, who was personally acquainted with the young hero, but lost his job as managing editor before the Y. H. came over, and in two weeks was installed on the payroll at $18 a week, which was approximately as much as he had ever earned in the ten years and a half of miscellaneous guerrilla warfare about the outskirts of the world of business and finance.

One year on The Georgian; then to The Kansas City Star, in the famed regime of Baron Nelson — the young hero went out to Kansas City on a Christmas vacation, wanted to see how The Star worked; The Star, per George Longan, city editor, wanted to see how he worked, if at all, and the job followed. First reporter on The Star to get a signed story; for years afterward was known as "DeWolf Hopper and I", from the theme of the first-personal narrative. Known by Monseigneur Diomede Falconio as his "Alter Ego" from the pertinacious manner in which the hero stuck to him on a tour in the Middle West when the Papal Legate was going about this country. Wrote hotels, zoos, personals, street-walkers — second raise was on a story starting,

"They would have been six little Magdalenes only they were not all repentant" — theaters, baseball, boxing and finally gold. Decided golf was a metier of the future and tried injudiciously to play it. Gave up playing about the time Alexa Stirling and Bobby Jones started. Removed from The Star to The Atlanta Georgian again and went in for golf heavily.

Left The Georgian by reason of an unsympathetic managing editor and took to the movies, which lasted four ungodly months with a personally conducted tour of Gloria Swanson to finish. Rushed back to the Fourth Estate in February, 1920, with The Atlanta Journal, where he will be until death them do part. Watched Alexa win three successive national golf championships and then took up Bobby Jones. Attended Bobby at twenty national championships and numberless lesser events. Watched him win seven major titles in the last five years after seven lean years in the past.

Author of "The Incomplete Golfer", based on his own experience; "Styles of Champions", "The Commonest Fault", and other more or less popular fiction and fact; "The Autobiography of an Average Golfer", printed serially in The American Golfer and then brought out in book form; and "Down the Fairway", done serially for a huge price for LIB-ERTY and then in book form, by the young hero and Bobby Jones in collaboration. Knighted by the Associated Press, July, 1926, for interview with Bobby Jones after the latter had won the British Open and the United States Open championships in 17 days. Since then, ready to die at any moment.

Fads — Trapshooting and aviation. Certainly not golf. Can fly a plane but not run a motor car.

Orders — Mason. Military Order of the Loyal Legion. Merry Meads of Wales. Fleas. Field Mice.

Clubs — Atlanta Athletic Club. Druid Hills Golf Club, El Quistador, Valparaiso, Fla. International Club of the Niagara Frontier. And some others.

As a young man, Keeler had double lumbar pneumonia and was *"snatched from death feet first"* by Dr. W. H. Perkinson of Marietta. He later developed inflammatory rheumatism in his left knee in 1917 which, despite Dr. Michael Hoke's treatments, left him stiff-legged for life. He thereafter "wheeled" his leg around in an awkward movement sometimes satirized by Jimmy Demeret and Jimmy Thompson in the Augusta National locker room in later years. As the players gathered there to change shoes, a "plant" (stooge) would poke his head inside and shout, "Jones is 2 under at the turn." Immediately, Thompson would play the role of Pop and stiffen his leg while wheeling it around vaudeville style as if to rush out on the course and pick up Bob's back nine action. Demeret, meanwhile, followed behind like a bobbing penguin just like the pigeon-toed Granny Rice used to move. The skit usually brought a chuckle.

Pop also suffered from calcium deposits in the leg muscles. He became a famous and frustrated hypochondriac. Pop took any and all home remedies offered on the theory that they might help him as well as the next person. His disposition vacillated from sunshine to gloom, and seldom was the downside not also accompanied by uproarious humor. Pop simply loved doctors and hospitals and illness of all sorts. He was repeatedly accused of contributing more to the financial welfare of the medical profession than any other living person. His schedule more often than not called for a visit to the doctor or dentist, and he used to "get in shape" for the ordeal of these visits.

Pop should at least be on the short list of all nominees for greatest practical joker among uncommon men. Before Pop met Bob Jones, Fuzzy Woodruff and Pop worked together at the city desk. As Pop fancied himself quite the golfer, he often kept his clubs in the office. Once Fuzzy encouraged Pop to demonstrate his new driver in the crowded newsroom. Fuzzy obtained an egg which was fixed to the floor with chewing gum as a "tee." On top of the egg was placed a golf ball. Fuzzy then bet Pop a quarter that he couldn't take a full swing and hit the golf ball without breaking the egg. If Pop ever turned down a proper bet, it was never recorded in a published report. Perhaps Pop never took so full a swing, for the one which followed smashed the egg and ball together, spraying the egg's contents all over the newsroom. Fuzzy reported: *"If a restaurant owner could spread an egg that far he could retire in six months."*

Egg was seen dripping from the ceiling, four walls, the clothes of all the wide-eyed staff, and all over the copy desk. The remainder was splattered on the countenance of the newspaper owner, Fred L. Seeley, who happened up the stairs at the penultimate moment to impact. Seeley was not persuaded that a story was in the making over the experiment, and the matter was simply dropped like a stone.

Another day, Pop brought to the office a pistol designed to shoot signal flares. The huge barrel could hardly be held with a single hand, but Pop insisted in demonstrating his skills to the fellow reporters. As O.B. was intently concentrating on sighting the gun, he did not realize that a Western Union boy was coming up the stairs to the City Room to deliver the day's messages. It is also likely that the messenger did not expect to be looking down the barrel of the largest pistol in captivity. Seemingly unaware, Pop kept up his dissertation in the art of aiming his pistol, and soon the messenger came face to face with the weapon wielded by Pop. As the eyes of the messenger dilated to the size of saucers, Pop blurted out "BANG!" at the top of his voice. The messenger passed out cold.

Pop was also an expert at helping a fellow reporter pack a fast suitcase for a prompt departure for the bus station. One early evening in Augusta, the 1938 Masters golf tournament had freshly been concluded. Fellow reporter Henry McLemore was frantically packing his bags on the eighth floor of the Bon Air Vanderbilt Hotel in hopes of making a bus ride to Jacksonville in about 35 minutes, when Keeler happened into the room.

Pop surveyed the situation and persuaded Henry that he should quickly go downstairs and check out while Pop helped pack his bags. O.B. assured McLemore, *"When you get back you won't have anything to worry about."* Henry reached the front desk, but he noticed that his bags never caught up with him. He did not then appreciate Pop's philosophy that "clothes do not make the man." Pop had taken all of McLemore's suitcase and wardrobe and carefully deposited them down the elevator shaft of the hotel! Pop reassured Henry there was no need for worry about luggage or clothes, *"Furthermore, there'll be more room on the bus now that you have no luggage. Your fellow bus riders will be more comfortable. You will be more comfortable yourself. For the service I have just rendered you I will not ask one penny in payment, for you see, Henry, you're an old and dear friend of mine and friendship knows no bounds."*

Pop could always invent a way out of a situation. One Thursday morning Pop was ready for work, until a torrential downpour threatened to prevent him from a prompt arrival at the Journal office. With his wife, Mommer, visiting North Carolina and no street car within easy reach of his home at Distillery Hill, Keeler tried calling the taxi company whose line rang busy for 40 minutes. Finally, with deadlines approaching on two pistol stories and a rifle story, Pop desperately called Western Union. He asked, *"Do you deliver persons to work?"* In a sincere effort to oblige, a messenger boy on a bicycle soon arrived and put Keeler in a rain-proof sack, threw him over his shoulders, and made haste to promptly deposit Keeler at The Journal door in time to meet his deadline!

Whenever the opera came to town, Pop got into the middle of the action. A dear friend was the great tenor, Enrico Caruso. After a night on the town, both Pop and Caruso ambled into Caruso's hotel lobby at about 4:00 a.m. The night clerk was the sole observer of Pops' next challenge, *"Rico, there's one thing I want you to do for me sometime. Just for me alone, I want you to sing a solo from my favorite opera."* Caruso replied, *"Well O.B., what's better than now?"* Caruso took a firm posture on the bottom of the staircase. Soon after, Caruso's magnificent voice resonated throughout the hotel. The awakened guests clicked open their locked doors and entered the hallways in robes and slippers to listen until the master was done. By that time the hotel stair-railing was populated with guests, all enthralled with the impromptu Caruso's performance. The Pied Piper Keeler smiled his approval.

Pop was widely sought as a speaker if not master of ceremonies at public functions. Upon the 60th anniversary of Grantland Rice's career, Pop remarked, *"A good toastmaster makes his own remarks so dull that by comparison the speeches sound brilliant. But I don't think I can do it with this bunch."*

At another event in Atlanta, Pop told the story of reporting on an Augusta tennis tournament accompanied by interested spectator Tyrus Raymond Cobb.

Ty Cobb had become interested in the progress of his son who had taken up tennis. During one match, the official called a ball out which had hit the line. A mild protest ensued. The player who had benefited by the questionable call then intentionally hit the next ball into the net to even the score for what the players informally believed to be an unfair call by the official. Cobb asked Keeler, *"Why did he do that?"* Keeler explained that tennis was a most civilized game, and the etiquette of the game called for justice. Cobb was indignant and made known his disgust over the situation. Pop then asked Cobb, *"What would happen if a baseball player slid into second base and was called safe and then got up and told the umpire his decision was wrong and that he had indeed been tagged out?"* Ty calmly and deliberately replied, *"There would be three deaths. First the umpire would drop dead, and then the manager of the player who protested would die."* The puzzled Keeler said, *"But that only makes two deaths."*

"Yes," said Cobb, *"but before he died the manager would take a bat and kill the player."* [79]

Pop was very handy with philosophy that was contained in one-liners or sometimes lengthier explications on life:

Matrimony is like a batter in baseball. The wife is the pitcher, the husband is the catcher. The wife gives the signals, the husband catches all the foul tips on his shins and finger joints. And when the box score is announced, all of the batters errors are passed balls and there are no wild pitches.

* * *

Pop's usual greeting to complete strangers who were beautiful females was, *"I love you madly; shall we flee together?"*

* * *

Work is the curse of the drinking classes (after Oscar Wilde)

* * *

I can resist anything but temptation

Once the "morning after," a lovely lady asked Pop for the poem he had kindly promised to write the prior evening. Keeler promptly sat and typed out the following:

I've indicted a petit jury, On the light in your eyes so fair;

And I've written a lovely lyric, On the glint in your golden hair;

And my typewriter's most ambitious, To ensure your lasting fame;

But the "likker" we had was vicious, And I can't remember your name.

Pop could certainly tell a story as well as create one. One favorite focused on Atlanta real-estate businessman George Adair and his son Perry, who was a Southern Amateur Champion and known as the original "Dixie Whiz Kid" in reporting circles. George hied himself to Montgomery to play an amateur tournament with Bobby Jones and other amateurs.

Adair met Bob's dad, Col. Robert P. Jones in the clubhouse enjoying a drink. The colonel was well known for his convivial nature and liberal use of profane language. The puckish Adair offered his friend a bit of advice for the next day's match. *"Bob I want you to be careful tomorrow morning about your language, because you have drawn a minister as your opponent."* The Colonel howled, *"Hell's bells! Now you have taken all the fun out of the tournament for me!"* Unbeknownst to the Colonel, the "word" was also slipped to his opponent that the Colonel was a minister. When the match was played, the Colonel, however, held his composure while his adversary cracked under the pressure on the seventh hole. Out of his mouth spewed forth a formidable combination of profanity, even for the golf course. The Colonel looked at him with absolute astonishment, *"I am amazed at you. I don't think a minister ought to talk like that."* The fairly enraged opponent shouted back *"Minister!! I'm no minister! Where on earth did you get that idea?"* The Colonel answered, *"But George Adair told me last night you were a minister!"* Having discovered the truth about each other's true identities, both the colonel and his friend played the remainder of the match with shots well spiced with their worst epithets. They repaired thereafter to the clubhouse and got roaring drunk together.

Keeler himself suffered frustration on the course when, for example, he played with Ed Danforth at East Lake one afternoon. Coming to the 15th hole, Pop was fairly on the green but needed four putts from 30 feet to get his ball down. As he looked up Pop spied a robin hunting for worms on the edge of the green. He exclaimed, *"Holy cow, how can a man putt with robins stomping around!"* Pop later came to the 18th hole needing a par 3 for a total of 97 for the round. The hole required a shot over water the entire distance to the hole. Pop topped his remaining three balls into the lake. Danforth then followed with all his remaining balls into the lake. Danforth next threw his 2-iron, which had failed him on the shots, into the lake. Pop then drew his 2-iron and threw it in as well. Then the players looked at each other, and without comment, alternately threw in each of their remaining clubs. Although Keeler made a move as if to throw his caddy in, Danforth intervened and "saved the lad." The two players then assuaged their wounded psyches in the clubhouse with liberal liquid refreshments.

After Bob Jones retired from competition, Pop accompanied him to Hollywood and narrated the 18 movie reels on golf techniques. In later years, Keeler continued to write about the new golf stars including Babe Zaharias, Joyce Wethered, Maureen Orcutt, Glenna Collett, Dorothy (Dot) Kirby, and Louise Suggs. Pop commented on women wearing shorts while playing golf:

To date I have not seen any important golf championships male or female, won in shorts. But then I have never seen any swimming records set in long pants either. [85]

Pop added to his international popularity with such lines as:

Far be it from me to assume the least of poking fun at our sedate and altogether sports-manlike British cousins, but in light of Miss Joyce Wethered's recent victory in the British ladies golf championship at St. Andrews, the suggestion forcibly obtrudes itself, that they might do a lot worse than induce Miss Wethered to enter the next British open championship, which the American forces have been capturing with such monotonous regularity since 1920.

Attending a women's golf tournament on one occasion, Pop said he noticed one of the players, whom he knew casually, was making a mistake in her swing causing damage to her score. At the lunch break he happened to be seated at her table, and he thought it might be helpful if he told her how to correct the situation.

He thought she would be grateful for the help. But no. She took it the wrong way. She said, *"Mr. Keeler, what do you know about golf? You can't play golf."*

That hurt Pop's feelings, and he said to the lady, *"You are entirely right, I can't play golf and I can't lay an egg, but I am a better judge of an egg omelet than any hen you ever saw."*

In his later years Pop recognized the changes in golf and noted:

The scoring is definitely improved although the golfers are not better. Their clubs are much better with the change from the wooden to the steel shafts being the main factor, they use the sand-wedge which they didn't used to, and the rough no longer is rough. Those three things have had a terrific effect on the scoring. Not only in men's golf but women's too.

* * *

Golf has changed as much as baseball, the changes brought about mainly through better equipment. Matched clubs with steel shafts have played a vital part in improving the game. Nowadays, it isn't necessary for a golfer to have a variety of shots. He has a club for every shot and need only judge distance. When Chick Evans won the title in 1916 he had seven clubs. Now the players have 14.

However, I don't want to leave the impression that these young fellows aren't as good as the old timers. They have made a study of putting and today that is where the championships are won.

In 1935 at the Charleston Open, Pop was hit in the back of the head by a golf ball. It required four stitches to close the wound. *"I'll never forget that round,"* he said holding his hand to the bandage *"In all of my 40 years, I've never been so struck by a golf shot."*

Pop got himself struck by the ball because his attention was diverted by a spectator who was pouring out his heart to him over a string of bad luck he was having. As Pop was beginning to "come around" a little, he said, *"Hit me again, I can still hear him."*

In 1938 Pop accompanied Charlie Yates, Watts Gunn, Tommy Barnes, and several other amateurs out West from Banff Canada to tournaments in Los Angeles. The train tickets were folded together like an accordion and unfolded all the way to the ground when held by one hand. After Charlie Yates had been to the drug store one day, he reported to Pop that he had weighed himself. *"How much did you weigh?"* asked Pop. *"One hundred fifty pounds,"* said Charlie. *"Stripped?"* asked Pop. *"No,"* Charlie answered, *"the drug store was too crowded."*

Pop wrote mostly under the by-line "O.O.'s by O.B." This stood for "once overs by O.B." and indicated Pop's intent to go over the sporting event after reviewing his notes. He also published "Out of Keeler's Golf Bag" and "This Game of Golf."

His first assignment, which started it all for Pop by earning him his first by-line on page one, was a report on a revival by a Billy Sunday-type preacher named the Rev. Len Broughton. Keeler was easily able to communicate the electric oratory on "religious therapeutics" to his readers. Stiles A. Martin, a fellow writer, watched in astonishment as City Editor Dudley Glass handed O.B. his copy of the "First-run" off the press in the press-room of the Atlanta Georgian.

The next year, Keeler went to the Kansas City Star where he rubbed shoulders with fellow reporter Ernest Hemingway. On April 16, 1912, Pop wrote a story which has served through the years as the model for journalism classes on how to effectively communicate with readers.

"The Titanic took 1,300 down!"

That was what the broad and heavy black headlines said and it was as if the morning papers came to the waiting doors bearing with them a knot of crepe.

"The Titanic took 1,300 down!"

There was a sound in the line as of a bell of death tolling somewhere — somewhere out on the broad Atlantic, a thousand fathoms above the sodden, twisted wreck of what had been earth's proudest ship.

"The Titanic took 1,300 down!"

Breakfasts were left untouched after the unfolding paper left bare the hideous intelligence. There was a hush in the street cars; a suggestive quiet in the subdued greetings at the offices; a dearth of laughter; so that the light unconsciously merry voice of an unthinking child jarred and somehow hurt in the burdened atmosphere of gloom.

"The Titanic took 1,300 down!"

Under the settled melancholy that terrible line hammered away at the imagination with a ceaseless irritation.

How did they meet it, this fearful thing? What did the men do, called on to face a ghastly death in the cold hours before dawn? Were they calm and steady, or were they a shrieking, merciless mob, fighting for places in the lifeboat? Did they help the women and children to places of safety with cheerful, comforting words that it was only a precaution — that nothing much was wrong — as men should who face the end as men? Or was the shame of La Furgoyne on their last moments — the beating off of women from the crowded boats; the maniacal rage of fear?

Brief as the last dispatches were, they showed there were heroes on the doomed ship.

The survivors were mostly women and children the dispatches said.

And there in that single line is as fine an epitaph as could be written for the men passengers and crew who went down with the ship. That line tells of a captain with his first and last thought for the passengers in his care: of a crew that made ready the lifeboats with never a hint of delay, and sent them clear of the foundering vessel with business-like precision unshaken by the doom their experienced eyes saw only too well.

That line tells of the manhood of Great Britain and America, almost buried, it seems at times, in the sordid struggle of an unromantic and unheroic age, yet flashing out as brightly at the grim need as ever it shown when knighthood was in flower.

The survivors were mostly women and children!

It is the brightest line of all that grim story: the stirring martial chord in the terrible dirge beginning:

"The Titanic took 1,300 down!"

After three years Pop returned to the Georgian in 1913. That year Pop wrote about the trial and conviction of Leo Frank, who was charged in the strangling death of Mary Phagan, an employee in a pencil factory of which Frank was the manager. Frank was found guilty and sentenced to death.

In the course of the next two years, Frank's sentence was commuted to life imprisonment by Gov. John Slaton, and in 1915 he was lynched.

Pop, of course, had covered the Frank story — from the trial to the commutation proceedings and the lynching — and late in the afternoon following the lynching, Frank's wedding ring was delivered to Pop at his home in Marietta. In addition to the ring, there was an unsigned note saying it was Frank's wish that the ring be delivered to his wife and asking Pop to do so.

Pop's son, George, was 10 1/2 years old at the time and remembers the incident quite well.

George said, *"We were living on Polk Street at the time, and sitting on the front porch when this man walked into the front yard.*

"Pop went down the steps to meet him. The man asked, 'Are you O.B. Keeler?' Pop said, 'Yes.' The man handed Pop an envelope, turned and walked slowly away.

"Pop took the envelope into the dining room where there was a light over the table. He opened the envelope and the ring and note fell out."

George was asked when and how Pop found the body.

"Well," George said, *"the night before the ring was delivered, the paper called Pop and told him a group of men from Cobb County had taken Frank from the state prison in Milledgeville and was going to hang him over Mary Phagan's grave in Marietta — and for Pop to get out there and wait for them.*

"Pop went to the cemetery, and when daylight came and nothing happened, he went to the courthouse where a farmer who had just arrived said, 'Something is going on out there at Frey's Gin.'

"That's how Pop 'found out' about the body."

Asked about speculation as to whether or not Pop knew the man who delivered the ring and note, George said, *"If Pop had known the man, the man would have known Pop and would not have asked him if his name was O. B. Keeler."*

In 1919 Pop wrote an obituary about the tragic deaths of two brothers, Mack and Jack, ages 11 and 9. The boys had dug a cave in the red Georgia clay of a bluff near their home. The cave collapsed on the boys and suffocated them. Pop reported that the boys likely were engaged in digging the cave while pretending to be fighting the Germans against invasion. Pop's theme was that the boys died as heroes in defense and love of their country. He wrote:

I guess Mack and Jack saw German trenches just across Bonaventure Avenue. The terrain is good for that sort of thing anyway. I can hear the older boy telling his brother that they will put one over the Huns — dig out their trench under the street, and put a big bomb under the wretched botches on the other side. They'd show 'em.***It was boys like Mack and Jack, grown up, that did show 'em too. Never forget that.

*   *   *

Looking at it one way, can't you see that Mack and Jack died for their country too--in the trenches for this country? In this trench at Bonaventure they were fighting the ghostly Germans across the way. And out of their trench at Bonaventure the brothers set forth together on the biggest adventure of all: the biggest adventure that comes to any of us, whether in France or Flanders or under the Red Old Hills of Georgia.

The mother of Mack and Jack was Eleanor McAuliffe. She was so moved by Keeler's story that they became acquainted and in 1927 were married.

Keeler's obituaries were extraordinary pieces of writing. He often fashioned the theme *"Game Called — Darkness"* to signal the close of a great person's life. Pop's obit on Babe Ruth was such a classic:

...The American baseball fans now and from now on, will remember Babe Ruth, not as vanishing in the darkness as a game is called, but striding across the home plate, and lifting his cap, and taking a homerun bow, with the sun on his face — to the "roar of the crowd."

Pop's obit on best friend Fuzzy Woodruff could be equally applied to his own career and life:

So far as I know his equal has never lived for the blazing ideal that he saw always in the long distance — and his invincible scorn of everything that was small, or petty or narrow or ugly. The man had a tremendous gift with language. He could write with anyone, especially when aroused. But no words of his, and surely no poor words of mine, can express the majesty of Fuzzy Woodruff's attitude toward life, which treated him none too well, but from which he wrung in less than half a century every thrill and every sensation that may be gained by an honorable gentleman who cast into the strife, plays out the game as a sportsman should.

Fuzzy Woodruff, a man of action if there ever lived one, goes from us in the midst of the sporting tumult that he loved. A soldier and a gentleman: a cavalier of life — the Fourth Musketeer — the eternal D'Artagnan has gone to his death like that other D'Artagnan on the field of battle the baton of a marshal of France in his hand. He died in the harness, and surely he says with Cyrano de Bergerac:

Tonight, when I enter God's house, one thing I carry with me, unblemished and unbent — I sweep the threshold with a snow-white plume.

✶　✶　✶

He never missed a story did Fuzzy Woodruff. The genius of the Fourth Estate was in his soul; and when we were together on the Atlanta Georgian he fairly made me a reputation as a writer by the lines he set above my stories.

He was known more widely and more thoroughly than any other newspaperman of his time. On the front page of the Kansas City Star during the war, the Star's own correspondent wrote of how he stumbled into a dugout one night lost among the front-line trenches and found there three American doughboys from Alabama. And as soon as he told them he was a newspaperman, they asked him in a chorus: "Do you know Fuzzy Woodruff?"

BOBBY JONES' SECRET WEAPON — O. B. KEELER

As with his friends Bob Jones and even Fuzzy, Pop Keeler, too, had genius in his soul. Pop *"succeeded admirably"* in the words of H.G. Salsinger of the Detroit News, *"in helping make the name of Jones one of the great ones in sport history. Incidentally, like the well-known Boswell, he helped himself to fame while doing it."* Pop himself oftentimes would say: *"I didn't give myself the worst of it, either."* Nor did his rich legacy give us any less.

Chapter 5
Forging a Champion's Record

SPALDING'S
ATHLETIC LIBRARY

Price 35 cent

Golf Guide

1925

PLAYING RULES of the U. S. G. A.

Edited by GRANTLAND RICE

BOBBY JONES
NATIONAL AMATEUR CHAMPION

AMERICAN SPORTS PUBLISHING COMPANY
45 ROSE STREET NEW YORK

At the 1925 U.S. Open in Worcester, Massachusetts, Bob had a great battle with Old Man Par and Willie MacFarlane and lost to both of them. During the first round of the championship, Bob's ball moved in the long grass on the steep bank at the side of the 11th green as he addressed it. Bob insisted, over objection of USGA officials, that a penalty stroke be added to his score. When praised for his honesty, Jones responded, *"You just might as well praise me for not breaking into banks. There is only one way to play this game."* Bob began the final round in fourth place and was able to tie MacFarlane. In the playoff round, Jones made the mistake of forgetting Old Man Par and went to playing Willie. Jones tried to get home with his second shot on an uphill hole of 555 yards and gain a psychological advantage. He made a critical bogey instead.

Bob shares the tee with Francis Ouimet, who beat Harry Vardon and Ted Ray in a playoff to win the 1913 U.S. Open. Ouimet was only able to win his second U.S. Amateur in 1931 after Jones retired the prior year. Herbert Warren Wind recalled: *"Once when I was talking with Francis Ouimet, an altogether modest and gracious man, about the long interval between his first victory in the Amateur, in 1914, [sic] and his second victory in 1931, he raised his voice to a dramatically emotional level, which was most unlike him, and said, "Don't get me wrong, but I played some pretty darn creditable golf in the Amateur in the twenties, then I'd run into Bobby, and he would absolutely annihilate me. You have no idea how good Bobby was!"*

The only time two members from the same club have ever met in the finals of a major championship occurred when Watts Gunn met Bob Jones in the 1925 U.S. Amateur at Oakmont in Pittsburgh. On the first tee, Watts asked Bob if he was going to give him his usual two shots per side, as was the custom during friendly matches in Atlanta. Bob looked Watts in the eye and retorted, *"I'm going to give you Hell you little s.o.b.,"* and he promptly proceeded to do so, dispatching Watts 4 and 3.

On the day before the final match, Watts secured a date from the gallery following him. As he slipped out of his room that night, he was *"collared"* by Bobby Jones. *"I was just going out for a bite to eat and I will be right back,"* said Watts. *"Oh no you won't,"* said Bobby. *"I am going to lick the hell out of you tomorrow and I don't want you to have any excuses when I do."* O.B. Keeler was assigned to stand watch over Watts the rest of the evening. Yet another follower in Watts' gallery later became Mrs. Jane Gunn.

FIFTEEN CENTS

TIME

The Weekly News-Magazine

VOL. VI. No. 9

ROBERT TYRE JONES JR.
"At grips with the invisible"
(See Page 27)

AUGUST 31, 1925

In July 1904, the Atlanta Athletic Club (AAC), founded in 1898, purchased 187 acres including a 30-acre lake for the building of the East Lake Country Club. Architect Tom Bendelow designed a seven-hole course which was later expanded to nine holes. In 1913, George Adair and Stewart Maiden toured England and Scotland and returned to revise the Bendelow course to the 18-hole modern No. 1 layout. The second and seventh holes had a par of 4-1/2. The original 1908 clubhouse was destroyed by fire in 1914 and completely rebuilt the following year.

Col. Robert P. Jones, Bob's dad, was on the AAC's Board of Directors from 1908 to 1946 and was club President from 1937 to 1942. Bob was President in 1946.

The 1925 fire not only consumed Bob Jones' 1925 U.S. Amateur trophy but also all of his golf clubs except the original Calamity Jane putter. In October 1929, Bob was playing East Lake when a Georgia thunderstorm struck. *"First a bolt of lightning hit the ground about twenty yards away from where we were standing. I felt the shock, and it made my shoulder tingle. One of the bunch suggested we go over to a clump of trees on the thirteenth for a spell, and we started on over, but the lightning beat us to it and just blew them to pieces. I thought I'd go on back to the clubhouse after that, and I did. Just as I got here the lightning struck the chimney and knocked all the bricks off. Three of them came right through the big umbrella I was carrying. One of them tore the sleeve right out of my shirt."* Fragments of the chimney were found a hundred feet away on the eighteenth green.

SPALDING'S

ATHLETIC LIBRARY

Price 35 cents

Golf Guide

1926

BOBBY JONES, National Amateur Champion

PLAYING
RULES
of the
U. S. G. A.

Edited by
GRANTLAND RICE

AMERICAN SPORTS PUBLISHING COMPANY
45 ROSE STREET, NEW YORK

ROBERT TYRE JONES, JR.
FOURTH FLOOR HAAS-HOWELL BUILDING
ATLANTA 3, GEORGIA

October 31, 1961

P. A. Ward-Thomas, Esq.
The Guardian
192 Grays Inn Road
London W. C. 1, England

Dear Pat:

Thanks so much for your letter. It was so good to see you, but as you say, our visit was much too brief.

I cannot help being saddened by what you tell me of the changes in turf conditions at Lytham. I know I was shocked to observe the same changes at St. Andrews. If this sort of thing is happening to all British sea- side golf, then indeed, progress has been dearly bought.

When the Open was played at St. Anne's a few years ago, it was obvious that something had happened to make it play much easier. I had thought at the time that this was no more than rain and an unaccustomed stillness. Apparently, this was not so.

Although I did not feel this way in the beginning, I am happy now that I did not miss playing seaside golf when the greens were hard and unwatered and the fairways and putting surfaces like glass. Nothing resulting from man-made design can equal the testing qualities of such conditions.

Please remember me most warmly to your charming wife.

With best regards,

Sincerely,

Bob

RTJ:jsm

During the fifth round of the 1926 British Amateur at Muirfield, Bob defeated the defending British Amateur champion, Robert Harris, 8 and 6. Of this match Keeler wrote: *"I had seen him go out and play par golf like a machine and crush his opponents with a ruthless pressure, but I never before saw him flame with the brilliancy he displayed against the luckless Scotsman. It was the first time an American and British champion had ever met in either country's championship and Bobby went out and destroyed Harris most spectacularly."*

Perhaps the finest round of golf ever seen in Great Britain was played by Bobby Jones at the Sunningdale Golf Club in Surrey, not far from London on June 16, 1926, in the qualifying round for the British Open Championship. Jones shot a 66: 33 on the front, 33 on the back, 33 putts, and 33 shots. Charlie MacFarlane of the *News* remarked, *"The boy's game was perfect and chaste as Grecian statuary."* Jones' total of 66-68 set a new record in the qualifying rounds for the British Open. Bob Jones is shown driving from the 13th tee.

In the 1926 British Open Championship at Royal Lytham and St. Annes, Bob is driving from the Eighth tee. Bob came to the 17th hole tied with Al Watrous. Jones' approach to the 17th green from the bunker on the left of the fairway was so expertly judged that *"a teaspoon too much of sand would have ruined the shot."* The ball finished inside Watrous' ball on the green. Watrous was so staggered that he three-putted to go 1 down coming into the home hole.

Bobby Jones sinking a 30-inch putt for a par 4 on the 72nd hole to settle the 1926 British Open Championship. Al Watrous and 15,000 fans look on.

The 1926 British Open champion at Royal Lytham and St. Annes. On the left is Norman Boaz of the Royal & Ancient Golf Club of St. Andrews. Walter Hagen is seen smiling over the champion's shoulder.

GEORGIA—MARCHING THROUGH! NEW YORK! Turn about is fair play, and certainly New York was good to Bobby Jones, the young golf hero from Dixie, as he led the parade, Major John S. Cohen, on his right, and Commissioner Joe Johnson, on his left, through the resounding lane of Broadway.
—Photo by Acme

...accept ...sho didn't ...the reception ...who was ...top deck of the ...just after leaving the Aquitania, they were lined up to face the camera ...ing from the left: R. T. Jones, of Canton, Bobby's grandfather; R. P. Jones, ...his father; Mrs. R. T. Jones, his grandmother; Mrs. Bobby Jones; Bobby ...ing a bit solemn, and Mrs. R. P. Jones, his mother. —Photo by Acme

NEW YORK AND ATLANTA JOIN IN WELCOME TO BOBBY JONES

THEY BOTH LOOK HAPPY, CERTAINLY
—Mr. and Mrs. Robert Tyre Jones, Jr.
—Underwood & Underwood

"IF YOU EVER GET INTO ANOTHER BUNKER, TRY THIS ONE!" urged Walter Hagen presenting a giant niblick to the new British open champion just before he gets the historic cup. —P. & A. Photos

...HE RETURNING HEROES OF THE GREAT INVASION AND ...O GREETED THEM. Left to right: R. P. Jones, Bobby's father; ...o, America's most famous professional; Watts Gunn, of Atlanta, ...tar; Al Watrous, the young professional who fought that astounding ...bby and finished a close second; Major Cohen, representing Mayor ...ns, at the head of the Atlanta welcoming party; Bobby Jones; Scott ...dent of the Atlanta Athletic Club; and Joseph Johnson, former ...New York commissioner, who represented Mayor Walker for New ...boat party. —Underwood & Underwood

Above—
THREE MUSKETEERS OF AMERICAN GOLF WHO DID THEIR STUFF IN ENGLAND. Bobby Jones, the winner, and the first amateur in 29 years to achieve the title; and at the left Al Watrous, young professional, who was second, and Walter Hagen who was tied for third place.
—Underwood & Underwood

IF YOU FANCY THERE IS A WEARY LOOK IN BOBBY'S EYES, just try the job of being the first American amateur ever to win a British open championship. Norman Boase, chairman of the Royal and Ancient championship committee, looks a bit fagged himself. —P. & A. Photos

To the Left—
"IT'S ALL YOURS, BOBBY!" assures Mayor Jimmy Walker, referring to New York. Al Watrous (at the left) and Commissioner Johnson seem to feel that the hospitable mayor is just about right.
—Photo by Acme

JONES FUND FOR PICTURE IS NOW $745

John W. Grant Heads List of Prominent Donors Late Saturday.

BOBBY AND WATTS KEEN TO ESCAPE SPOTLIGHT'S GLARE

BY ANGUS PERKERSON
(Journal Staff Correspondent
NEW YORK, July 3.—After ...the central figures in one of ...York's greatest demonstration ...by Jones and Watts Gunn ...turn to the less exciting w ...golf by playing a 36-hole mat ...day over the Columbia cou ...Washington with Freddie M ...professional at Columbia, and ...MacKenzie, long-driving amat ...their opponents.

And it is no secret that he ...be glad to substitute golf fo ...tions. They appreciate dee ...wonderful welcome given th ...New York but neither likes t ...ter of the stage.

The speech by Watts Gunn ...dinner given to Bobby, Wat ...O. B. Keeler in the Delta ...room of the Vanderbilt, Friday ...testified to this. And Watts' ...because of its directness a ...cerity, was really the hit ...

"I'm just simply scared to ...he said, "and I think a dirt ...has been played on me by th ...master, or rather my fathe ...went off and left me here to ...speaking."

After that Watts continu ...making a speech, chiefly abo ...by, which delighted his audie ...Bobby and Watts plan to g ...New York to Washington ...afternoon, play in Washingto ...day, and then go to Columbus ...for the American open golf ...ment, which will be played ...Scioto Country club next Thu ...Friday and Saturday.

What Bobby Says

On his arrival Friday from ...head, Bobby, in answer to a q ...about the American open, sa ...golfer wins as I have done ...once in every six or seven ...That being so, I'm going to p ...less, I guess, just to play an ...a pleasant time."

Which was just Bobby's m ...He is going to play the best of ...he is capable, which is the b ...the world, and he will be the f ...of the critics to win, though ...is no picking winners in open ...tournaments.

...It is interesting to feel here h ...fine courtesy extended Jess Sw ...at first day night's banquet to

(Continued on Page 5, Colum

Tommy Armour, Harry Vardon, and Bobby Jones. Armour was responsible for teaching Jones the subtle genius of the Old Course at St. Andrews. Vardon taught Jones much about destiny and greatness.

Jones played Walter Hagen in a 72-hole match at Bob's home course, the Whitfield Estates Country Club in Sarasota, and Hagen's home course, the Pasadena Country Club in St. Petersburg. Hagen prevailed 12 and 11. H.W. Wind chronicled the *"crack that Walter had gone around in 69 strokes and Bobby in 69 cigarettes."* In his match with Jones, Hagen used 27 putts in the first round and 26 in the second. Jones took 31 putts in the first round and 30 in the second. Jones played the last 25 holes of the match in par and went 4 down to Walter's amazing golf. British golf writer A.C. Croome explained Hagen's method:

He makes more bad shots in a single season than Harry Vardon did from 1890 to 1914, but he beats more immaculate golfers because, 'three of those and one of them counts four,' and he knows it.

Frank Adair sits atop the 1925 five-gaited "World's Grand Champion" named Vendetta. Bob Jones attended the 1926 national horse show in Barbourville, Kentucky, sponsored by Kiwanis International. Barbourville was home to the T.W. Minton Company, which was a major supplier of Jones' hickory shafts. Minton was also a major supplier of baseball bat blanks to the H&B Company in Louisville, Kentucky, wheel spokes to the automobile industry, and walking canes worldwide.

Bob returned a score of 71 for the qualifying round of the National Amateur golf championship at Baltusrol Golf Club in Springfield, New Jersey, September 13, 1926. He was defeated in the final by George Von Elm 2 and 1. Von Elm was Jones' victim in the 1924 Amateur championship at Merion CC.

Jones' defeat by Von Elm at Baltusrol in 1926 would be the last 36-hole match Bob ever lost to an amateur. Jones had previously beaten Von Elm 9 and 8 at Merion and 7 and 6 at Oakmont. Jones dismissed his supporters who said the tournament was in the bag: *"Nobody is going to keep on beating a golfer as good as George Von Elm."* It was the first time a national championship trophy was taken west of the Rocky Mountains.

Scioto Country Club will be forever famous in golf history as the scene of one of Bob Jones' greatest victories.

USGA President William C. Fownes presents the 1926 Open championship trophy to Bobby Jones. Atlanta Athletic Club member Thomas C. Paine is at Bob's right. At the extreme right is Melvin Traylor, a Chicago banker who was the 1928 USGA president and later a founding member of the Augusta National Golf Club.

At the home hole, Jones was able to collect his birdie with the aid of a drive which measured 310 yards.

Bobby Jones with the 1926 U.S. Open Championship trophy. Bob was the first winner of the "Double," both the United States and British Open championships in the same year.

Bob's *"less than enthusiastic countenance"* in this photo could perhaps be explained by the excruciating stress visited upon him during the championship. At 7am on this day Dr. Earl Ryan had prescribed medication to quell the nausea which caused Bob to lose his breakfast.

Then after he finished play, and with the outcome still in doubt, Bob returned to his Neil House hotel room and let go of the pent-up pressure by sobbing uncontrollably. Minutes later he was telephoned to come out, accept the trophy and have his photo taken.

In September 1926, Bob Jones teamed with Tommy Armour against Leo Diegel and Gene Sarazen in the first match ever played on the links of the "magnificent" new Miami Biltmore Golf Club. Bob won the match. Jones and Armour prevailed in this match as part of a series of seven fourball matches against pairs of the best professionals in the country.

Price 35 cents

SPALDING'S
ATHLETIC LIBRARY

Golf Guide

EDITED BY
Grantland Ri[ce]

GEORGE
VON ELM
National
Amateur
Champion

ROBERT T. (Bobby) JONES, JR.
United States Open Champion
British Open Champion

MRS. G. HEN[RY]
STETSON
Women's
National
Cham[pion]

1927

Playing Rules of
the U.S.G.A.

AMERICAN SPORTS PUBLISHING COMPAN[Y]
45 ROSE STREET NEW YORK

The 1927 Southern Open champion at East Lake — Bob Jones.

Ralph McGill of the Atlanta Journal wrote of Jones: *"He is a man who never took himself or his feats seriously enough to stuff his shirt with them. Of them all, his feet are freest of clay, the man himself most devoid of guile, envy, false pride and over-riding ambition."*

The finish of a spade mashie shot at St. Andrews in 1927, where Bob successfully defended his British Open title.

Jones' approach to the last hole ended in the Valley of Sin, just short of the green. The learned Darwin next observed:

Thence he ran it up dead and as he scaled the bank the crowd stormed up after him and lined the edge of the green, barely restraining themselves. He holed his short one and the next instant there was no green visible, only a dark seething mass, in the midst of which was Bobby, hoisted on fervent shoulders and holding his putter 'Calamity Jane,' at arm's length over his head lest she be crushed to death.

An old Scot standing by the green muttered: *"The man canna be human."*

After being "chaired" to the Royal & Ancient clubhouse, Jones told the crowd of 12,000 that winning the championship on the Old Course had been the ambition of his life. He thanked the crowd for their kindness and stated that he was not going to take the trophy out of Scotland but would be pleased to leave it in the custody of the Royal & Ancient of which he was proud to be a member.

Mid-Week Pictorial

"NEWS OF THE ~~WORLD~~ IN PICTURES"

PUBLISHED WEEKLY
BY
THE NEW YORK TIMES
COMPANY

AUGUST 4,
1927
VOL. XXV, NO. 24

TEN CENTS

CANADA
15 CENTS

America's Wizard of the Links: Bobby Jones
With the British Open Championship Cup, Just After He Had Won It for the Second Consecutive
Year at St. Andrews With the Record Score of 285, After One of the Most Dazzling
Performances in Golf History. (Times Wide World Photos.)
The Earthquake in Palestine—Prince of Wales on His Canadian Ranch—American Cities: Charleston, S. C.—Sports—Theatres—Motion Pictures—Books—Fashions—Aviation.

Mid-Week Pictorial

"A National Magazine of News Pictures"

VOL. XXV, No. 25.   NEW YORK, AUGUST 11, 1927.   PRICE TEN CENTS

MISS JONES WELCOMES DADDY HOME: BOBBY JONES, AFTER WINNING THE BRITISH
OPEN GOLF CHAMPIONSHIP
for the Second Successive Year, Is Greeted on His Return to Atlanta, Ga., by His Daughter, Clara Malone
Jones, Aged 2 Years and 3 Months.

Perhaps Bob's favorite championship photograph following his 1927 U.S. Amateur victory at Minikahda after defeating Chick Evans 8 and 7.

Mid-Week Pictorial

"NEWS OF THE WORLD IN PICTURES"

TEN CENTS
CANADA
15 CENTS

SEPTEMBER 8,
1927
VOL. XXVI, NO. 3

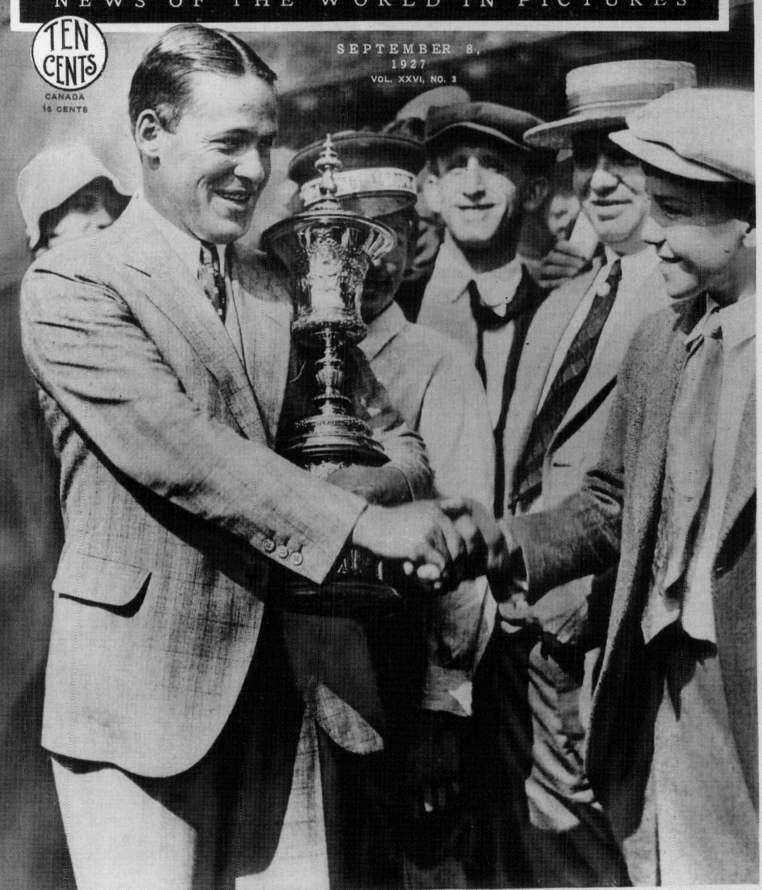

Greatest Golfer in the World: With the New Gold Amateur Cup,
Bobby Jones Returns to Atlanta and Is Greeted by Charlie Yates, a Junior Golfer of Great
Promise. Jones Has Now Won the American Amateur Title Three Times in Four Years

(Times Wide World Photos.)

Pacific Fliers at Honolulu—Golf and Tennis Championship Tournaments—Asbury Park Baby Parade—
American Cities: Tacoma—Sports—Theatres—Motion Pictures—Books—Fashions—Science

Defending U.S. Amateur champion Bob Jones defeated British Amateur champion T. Philip Perkins in the 1928 Amateur Championship at Brae Burn Country Club, West Newton, Massachusetts. Perkins commented, *"When one plays against Mr. Jones, he has only the pleasure of being defeated by the greatest of all golfers and the finest of all sportsmen."* At the close of 1928, Jones had been national champion six years in a row.

No. 3X   PRICE 35 CENTS

SPALDING'S
ATHLETIC LIBRARY

GOLF GUIDE
1929

PLAYING RULES OF THE U. S. G. A.

EDITED BY GRANTLAND RICE

AMERICAN
SPORTS
PUBLISHING
COMPANY

45 ROSE ST.
NEW YORK

The 33rd playing of the United States Open Championship in 1929 was at the west course of the Winged Foot Golf Club at Mamaroneck, New York, the last week in June 1929. Bob arrived early and spent eight days practicing on the course.

On the morning of the first day, Jones went out on the east course to warm up. After hitting a few successful drives, Bob dropped back to a No. 4 iron which was a club he used in practice as a *"sort of indicator to the prospective behavior of all its companions."* He hit shot after shot, trying everything he could think of, but all of them went to the right of the objective except a few that he tried to keep straight by a vigorous roll of the right hand. These shots were just as far off line in the other direction. T.N. Bradshaw of Atlanta, who made the trip with Bob, was watching his practice. "Brad" had played with "Rabbit" (only Bradshaw enjoyed the luxury of employing this diminutive) on numerous occasions and knew his game as well as anyone. *"I think you are playing the ball too far back, Bob,"* he said quietly. Bob did not agree with him but was in a humor to try anything. So he played the next few shots farther forward and from that time had no more trouble.

Bob's first round of 69 was also his first round under 70 ever in a U.S. Open. Rain slowed down the course, but Jones led after the third round by 3 over Sarazen and by 4 over Espinosa. Bob is shown here holing a putt on the ninth green.

During the final round, Bob was never more confident and serene in his life. He hit a good drive around the dogleg to the eighth hole and hit a good No. 4 iron second, which caught the edge of the bunker on the right corner of the green. It was an unlucky break because a yard more to the left and the ball would have finished close to the hole. Bob described his state of mind from there:

I felt that might be considered an unlucky break, but I had had several unlucky ones and anyway the bunker was not difficult. I would have a putt for a 4, and even if I failed to get it I could be out in 36 which was good enough. My shot out of the bunker was not bad either, but the green sloped away and was keener than I expected. The ball kept trickling and barely tumbled over the edge of another bunker this time in a nasty place under the bank. Anything might happen then. It did. Back across the green I went into the bunker I had just left, this time out successfully and two putts for a 7. Once having seen how easily it could be done, I became afraid of every second shot, afraid of going into another bunker. I tried to steer them all, and I got the usual reward for my pains. I have played the first 7 holes in 1 under 4s; I played the last 11, 2 under 5s. The first disaster was one of things that can happen anytime you lower your guard. The balance of the round was an agony of anxiety.

Coming to the last hole, Bob had a 4 to tie but pulled his pitch, and the ball rolled down the slope of a deep bunker at the left of the green stopping in the grass before it reached the sand where he is seen playing his next shot.

This villainous, curling, side hill 12-foot putt separated Jones from a tie with Al Espinosa for the 1929 U.S. Open Championship. O.B. Keeler could not bear to watch the *"all or nothing"* putt and simply listened to the crowd's reaction to learn the outcome. Keeler heard a *"thin click"* followed by a loud sigh which changed into a roaring thunderbolt when the putt went down. Grantland Rice pronounced it *"Golf's Greatest Putt."* Al Watrous described the putt to Keeler as so perfectly gauged that *"if the hole had been a 4¼-inch circle on the green, the ball would have stopped in the middle of it."*

Bob was inspired by making the 12-foot par putt which won a berth in the playoff with Espinosa. The large crowd milled about the clubhouse at the Winged Foot Golf Course in Mamaroneck, New York, on June 29 after Bobby Jones tied with Al Espinosa for first place in the U.S. Open Championship. During this time, Bob went to the USGA tent to find out what time he was scheduled to playoff with Al Espinosa the following Sunday morning. The match was set for 9:00 a.m. Bob then suggested, *"Why don't we start at 10:00? Al will probably want to go to Mass."* The time was changed. After a bad start with a bogey on the first hole, Jones played the best golf of the tournament, finishing the 36-hole playoff with 72-69-141. Espinosa, emotionally drained from suffering an 8 on the 11th hole the day before, finished 23 strokes in arrears.

Chapter 6
March on Britain

Bobby Jones and St. Andrews: what each meant to the other is one of the greatest love stories in the annals of golf.

Later in life, Jones conceded: *"I could take out of my life everything except my experiences at St. Andrews and I would still have a rich and full life."* The citizens of St. Andrews were no less extravagant in their appraisal of Jones. They adopted him, gave him his nickname *"Bobby,"* conferred citizenship upon him, named the 10th hole after him, eulogized him, and impressed his legend on the minds and hearts of all who cared to pass along the splendid history to others.

How it all happened is well worth recounting since it had such an inauspicious beginning.

1921

OPEN CHAMPIONSHIP

Centuries of golf history had been recorded by the time Bobby Jones first arrived at St. Andrews in 1921 as a young man of 19. Legions of golfing heroes had already earned the respect and admiration of perhaps the most knowledgeable golf citizenry in the world. Old Tom and Young Tom Morris had displayed their legendary skills on the Old Course links and were revered as beloved native sons. It was perhaps with high hopes that Jones traveled across the Atlantic Ocean on his maiden voyage to display his golf prowess on Scottish soil. Jones had acquitted himself with some aplomb at local amateur events in his native Georgia. He had even caused a stir worthy of mention at the 1916 U.S. Amateur in posting the low medal round.

Jones brought much talent and capability to St. Andrews in 1921. His swing mechanics were sound enough to justify the nickname *"Boy Wonder"* which the media had given him. The townspeople gave the golfing prodigy much respect after his opening round of 78. He was paired with eventual champion Jock Hutchison, a native St. Andrean and naturalized American. Hutchison was clearly the teacher in that round, with Jones in the front row seat. The veteran made a hole-in-one on the 142-yard eighth hole and nearly holed his drive on the next hole of 303 yards for a double-eagle. Hutchison finished with 72, six strokes less than Jones. In the afternoon, Jones played better and led the entire amateur field with an aggregate of 152.

Jones was positioned for low amateur runner-up honors if not for an act which veteran scribe Henry Longhurst noted *"would have quickly been forgotten if committed by an ordinary player."* Simply stated, Jones quit in mid-round and ended his inaugural pilgrimage in shame and disgust. He had played the outward half in what he deemed a shocking 46. His bad luck continued on the 10th hole (which later would be renamed in his memory) by making 6. At the short, par-3 11th - one of only two par 3s on the course - Jones hit his tee shot into Hill Bunker, which guards the left side of the green. Sand flew out on his second stroke, but unfortunately not the ball. He did the same on his third and fourth strokes, and perhaps the next, before he lost his composure. Reports of what transpired next are inconsistent. Either Jones left the bunker with the ball in his pocket or he picked up on the green before holing out. Even Jones himself later wrote contradictory accounts.

One of the few eyewitnesses to the spectacle was David Anderson, owner of the nearby Kinburn Hotel, who wrote to the editor of the St. Andrews Citizen in October 1958: *"Sir: I can remember seeing Bobby Jones tear up his card at the 1921 Open. It happened after Bobby had driven off from the 12th tee. Walking up the fairway, Bobby asked the marker for his card, after a short scrutiny, coolly and deliberately tore it to shreds. Only a handful of spectators were present at the time, certainly not more than a dozen, including the players and caddies in the party."*

The legendary golf writer Bernard Darwin erroneously reported that following the mishap at the 11th, Jones *"teed up his ball and drove it far away into the Eden."* As no writer witnessed the event, several inaccurate and conflicting reports were published, based only on hearsay.

Jones' earliest published account was five years later, in 1926, when he wrote that he had taken 46 strokes at the turn. Later, in his autobiography, Down the Fairway, he wrote that he turned in 46 and did not hit his ball into the Eden: *"I have some sterling regrets in golf. This is the principal regret - that ever I quit in a competition... But I was a youngster, still making my reputation. And I often have wished I could in some way offer a general apology for picking up my ball on the 11th green of the third round, when I had a short putt left for a horrid 6. It means nothing to the world of golf. But it means something to me. Much more now than it did six years ago, when I took 46 for the first nine of the third round, and a 6 at the 11th, and said to myself, 'What's the use?'*

"Of course I continued to play, after tearing up my card -that is a figurative term, by the way - and shot a very good 72 in the fourth round which would have put me in a decent position had I kept on in the competition. (Jones was not required to discontinue play after the incident.) But my showing is not to be mentioned prominently in the same tournament where Jock Hutchison made that tremendous finish, and Roger Wethered, the English amateur, by stepping inadvertently on his own ball, lost a stroke and the championship, going into a tie with Jock, who beat him in the playoff."

Jones' withdrawal from the 1921 Open was his only failure to complete a major championship which he entered. Perhaps the incident formed the basis for his resolve never again to breach the highest ethics of sportsmanship. He had already made great strides in *"taming his naturally fiery temperament"* by curbing a childish proclivity to throw clubs about.

Nevertheless, out of the ashes of Jones' first visit to St. Andrews, would rise the phoenix of a golf legend unequaled through the generations.

1926

WALKER CUP

During the five-year hiatus between his inaugural pilgrimage to St. Andrews and his return in 1926, young Jones did much studying both in the classroom and on the golf course. He earned his bachelor of science degree in 1922 from Georgia Tech and bachelor of arts in 1925 from Harvard. At the same time, he broke into the major championship ranks with victories in the 1923 U.S. Open (Inwood), 1924 U.S. Amateur (Merion) and 1925 U.S. Amateur (Oakmont). He also worked in the real estate business in Florida, where he was fortunate to spend time with Tommy Armour, the *"Silver Scot."* It was from Armour that he learned about the subtleties of the British links.

As was his custom, Jones rarely competed in any tournament other than a major championship. His 1926 schedule included three events in the British Isles: the Amateur at Muirfield, the Walker Cup at St. Andrews and the Open at Royal Lytham and St. Anne's - in that order.

As the reigning U.S. Amateur champion, Jones was favored to win the British version at Muirfield. But he lost in the sixth round to Andrew Jamieson of Glasgow. The winner was New Yorker Jess Sweetser, the first American-born golfer to capture the title. From Muirfield, the contingent of top American and British players traveled up the coast to St. Andrews for the Walker Cup.

Jones defeated the masterful Cyril Tolley in singles by a 12 & 11 margin in a 36-hole match. He also teamed with fellow Georgian Watts Gunn to conquer the duo of Tolley and Jamieson in foursomes play.

The Americans won the Walker Cup by the narrow margin of six matches to five. Jones originally planned to return home after the Walker Cup, but instead went south to England for the Open Championship at Royal Lytham and St. Anne's. His failure to win the Amateur at Muirfield and subsequent fine play in St. Andrews influenced his decision. Jones won the championship, becoming the first amateur to do so since Harold Hilton in 1897.

1927
OPEN CHAMPIONSHIP

Jones' interest in selling real estate waned in late 1926, and he enrolled at Emory Law School. The raw weather in Atlanta and demands of law school prompted him to put his clubs in the closet from about October until March.

In spite of the winter layoff, Jones began the golf season with a victory in the Southern Open Championship at his home course of East Lake. In the U.S. Open at Oakmont, he finished 11th - his worst of his eight appearances in the championship. (His friend Tommy Armour won that one.)

Up until then, Jones had absolutely no plans to go to St. Andrews to defend his British Open title. However, his disgust with his abysmal showing at Oakmont changed his mind. O.B. Keeler, Jones' biographer and publicist, learned of Jones' entry into the Open while on his way to Paris from New York City on a honeymoon. Keeler was able to add a side trip to St. Andrews and keep intact his record of being the only man to see Jones win all of his major championships.

Jones arrived in Glasgow on the ship Transylvania with only five days to prepare for the championship. His father, Col. Bob Jones, and several friends accompanied him. Although he lacked confidence in his game, he had no trouble qualifying with a record-tying round of 71 over the New Course.

Whatever uncertainties preceded the 1927 Open were swept away in Jones' spectacular opening round of 68. It was the first time he broke 70 in a major championship. After a wobbly start -requiring a 30-foot putt at the second for a bogey - Jones holed a 120-foot putt at the fifth for an eagle 3. He played the first nine holes in 32 and returned in 36, while taking only 29 putts in the round.

Jones led the championship wire-to-wire with succeeding rounds of 72, 73 and 72, for what he termed *"the amazing winning aggregate of 285."* Never before had such a low score been recorded in the national events of either Britain or America. It was, in effect, a one-man championship with Jones leading the field by six strokes after the first day and by the same margin at the end.

The spectators carried the champion on their shoulders all the way to his hotel, where his father was waiting. *"I'm mighty glad that's over,"* the younger Jones said with a laugh. The Colonel was extremely proud: *"I'd rather him win the title here than on any other course in the world and so would Rob."*

Jones received yet another great reception from the crowd when he went across to the Royal and Ancient clubhouse for the presentation ceremony outside the main entrance. His acceptance remarks reflected his unusual gift for international diplomacy. He said that winning the championship on the Old Course had been the *"ambition of his life."* He thanked the crowd for their kindness and stated that he would not take the trophy out of Scotland, but would be pleased to leave it in the custody of the R & A, of which he was proud to be a member. The cheers were deafening.

At the train station, Jones' father emphasized that British sportsmanship was a very real thing and that both he and his son had been overwhelmed by their reception. He spoke of how they deeply appreciated the spectators' traditional sense of admiration for the winner regardless of his nationality. This, despite the fact that his son had come over virtually a stranger and secured their title at a time when Britishers were making great efforts to regain it. This mutual admiration society would be blessed by an increase in membership in the forthcoming great year of 1930.

MARCH ON BRITAIN

1930
AMATEUR CHAMPIONSHIP

In the spring of 1930, Bobby Jones had one golfing goal on his mind. He wanted to capture the only championship which had always eluded his grasp: the British Amateur. Jones called it the most important tournament of his life.

Most winters, Jones hung up his clubs. This year, though, he competed in two winter "open" tournaments where he could enjoy heated competition against professionals. In spite of setting the course record twice with rounds of 67-65 in the Savannah Open, Jones still finished behind Horton Smith. He then played what he observed as the *"best golf I ever played in any tournament before or since"* in posting a 13-stroke victory in the Southeastern Open in Augusta.

The extra preparation paid off for Jones in Britain. His first competition was the Walker Cup at Royal St. George's in Sandwich, where he was playing captain. Jones kept his record flawless by defeating Roger Wethered, the highly regarded Englishman, by a score of 9 & 8 in a 36-hole singles match. Jones also won his doubles match as the United States denied Britain custody of the cup for the sixth straight time since 1922, when the matches began. He then competed in a one-day, 36-hole event at Sunningdale for the Golf Illustrated Gold Vase. Not surprisingly, he won.

Jones could not have been more confident in his game as he journeyed north to St. Andrews for the 41st British Amateur Championship. The format required eight 18-hole rounds of match play, followed by a 36-hole final.

Because of the abundance of short, one-round matches, it was not unusual for a favorite to be eliminated in an early round by a lesser player with a hot putter. This could have been the case in the first round had Jones not played superbly against Syd Roper from Nottinghamshire. Roper showed no fear in the opening holes, posting five 4s in succession for a 1-under-par streak. He even maintained his composure when Jones sank a 140-yard shot from the Cottage Bunker for an eagle 2 on the fourth hole. Roper's brave response was simply to halve Jones with a birdie 4 on the next hole. In spite of his strong play, Roper was 3-down after five holes as Jones opened 3-4-3-2-4.

Roper added only one 5 to 14 consecutive 4s as he finally succumbed to Jones' assault on the course record on the 16th green. (A pair of 4s on the remaining two holes would have tied the course record of 68.) Jones later commented that Roper's steady play would have demolished anyone else on the field.

The next morning, Jones easily dispatched Cowan Shankland 4 & 3 to set up a crowd-pleasing match with Cyril Tolley, the defending champion and two-time titleholder.

Thousands of spectators came for the match. Reporter Bernard Darwin observed that *"every man, woman and child in St. Andrews"* was on hand to see which titan of golf could master the gale that masqueraded as a *"fresh breeze."* It blew the sand out of the bunkers while spectators took refuge in the sand hills between shots. Every putt was painted with treachery and emphasized the need to measure not only the quickness of the surface but also the wind's effect.

None of Jones' matches at St. Andrews in 1930 would be decided by more than a couple of strokes. The match with Tolley was no exception. The battle seesawed, and the match came to the 17th all level. The stage was set for a controversy that still remains fodder for lively debate.

At the 17th, Tolley outdrove Jones slightly and was in a better position to avoid the deadly Road Bunker guarding the left of the steeply sloping green. Jones, from the left side of the fairway, was tempted with a daring shot to the flag over the same bunker, but resisted. He knew better.

His best recourse would be to play up the left side of the green, near the 18th tee, past the Road Bunker. He could then play an approach to the flag without hindrance of the notorious bunker. Before making his shot, Jones climbed a hillock and waved at the marshals to move the crowd back from the intended flight line. After he was satisfied that the crowd could move back no further, he hit a 4-iron on line, but a bit too strong. The ball flew into the crowd and was deflected back to the top edge of the green some 40 to 50 feet from the hole.

Some observers, particularly fans of Tolley, asserted that Jones' shot was intentionally played into the crowd. Jones insisted that his efforts to move the spectators back was proof that he never planned a ricochet against the crowd. (Regardless of Jones's intentions, rules officials decided thereafter that no part of a championship gallery should be allowed to the left of the green.)

Tolley pulled his second shot slightly and came to rest to the left of the green with the devilish Road Bunker intervening. It was not the place to be. At this point, a Jones two-putt appeared certain to win the hole. But Tolley pulled off a miracle with a deft pitch over the bunker. Accounts state that the pitch was *"bravely judged so that it trembled momentarily on the edge of the bunker before trickling down a foot from the hole."* In an unexpected change of events, Tolley appeared to be back in the match with a probable 4 for a halve. Then Jones left his approach putt some 8 feet from the hole. But he was relentless as his slippery putt fell into the hole to move the drama to the 18th, all even.

Jones later acknowledged that Tolley's third shot *"has never been surpassed for exquisitely beautiful execution."* Tolley himself agreed it was the finest shot of his life.

The 18th was also halved, taking the match back to the first hole with each player understandably exhausted. Tolley's second shot ended left of the green, and his chip was slightly closer to the hole than his opponent's 10-foot birdie putt. Even though the birdie attempt failed, Jones managed a stymie by obstructing Tolley's line to the hole and emerged the victor.

Jones retired George O. Watt of Monifieth in his fourth-round match by a margin of 5 & 4. In each of the following two matches, against American Jimmy Johnston and Scot Eric Fiddian, Jones was at one point 4-up. Even so, he needed to make an 8-foot putt at the home hole to turn back Johnston's late charge, and he needed a sub-par round to turn back Fiddian.

The semifinal match against fellow Walker Cupper George Voigt, from New York, was a different story. Jones broke with his tradition of waiting until all competition was completed before consuming an alcoholic beverage. Before the afternoon match Jones had a glass of sherry to calm his nerves. Mixed with his natural adrenaline, the wine's effect was multiplied. It wasn't until the match was in the latter holes before Jones could properly focus his blurred vision. By that time, Voigt had accumulated a seemingly convincing 2-up advantage with only five holes remaining to play. But on the 14th hole, Voigt fortuitously drove out of bounds, providing Jones the opening he needed. An onslaught of Jones' best golf thereafter gobbled up Voigt's lead until Jones secured victory on the home hole where Voigt tragically three-putted. (In the 13 matches Jones played that year in winning the British and U.S. Amateur titles, Voigt was the only player to have Jones more than 1-down.)

Jones' 36-hole final match was played on Saturday against Roger Wethered, the 1923 Amateur Champion and runner-up in the 1921 Open at the Old Course.

Enormous crowds gathered for the closing contest: about 6,000 persons in the morning and almost 15,000 in the afternoon. *"Motor cars streamed into the city from all quarters,"* the local newspaper reported. *"Thousands arrived by rail, and the various buses were packed."*

The match began with rather ordinary play and, although Jones was 1-up by the 10th hole, he was concerned with his putting accuracy. By the end of the morning round, his medal score of 71 gave him a 4-up advantage. But he admitted that he was far from comfortable.

Jones had what he termed a *"touch-and-go"* start in the afternoon. He was out in 37, Wethered in 38. The match concluded at the 12th with the margin at 7 & 6. Jones was 2-under 4s.

Wethered at once congratulated Jones on his deserved victory. then the surging crowd of cheering admirers surrounded Jones. The stewards and policemen struggled in the difficult task of escorting the champion on a half-hour journey from the links to his quarters at the Grand Hotel.

The champion, face drawn and haggard from the week's ordeal of matches, described his state: *"I don't think I was ever so happy about any golf event in my life... I was not confident with my putts today, but then Roger was missing them, and I began to feel that the difficult greens must have something to do with it... I've been lucky but I'm glad. I shall do my best at Hoylake [in the upcoming Open Championship] but I shall not worry if I do not win there. This was the big thing for me."*

The victor changed into a smart gray suit and made his way through the sea of spectators to the steps of the R & A clubhouse to accept the championship cup. The speeches were amplified by microphone and could be heard well beyond Granny Clark's Wynd (the road crossing the links) and from the windows of houses and hotels nearby. The first and 18th fairways were blanketed with thousands of exuberant spectators.

Col. P.G.M. Skene, captain of the R & A, remarked about the keenness of the play, especially the magnificent fight between Jones and Tolley. He then asked the champion to come and accept the trophy while stating that although the champion was from the other side of the Atlantic, they in St. Andrews could *"claim a bit of him as he was a member of the Royal and Ancient Club."*

After several minutes of thunderous applause and cheering, Jones observed: *"I must say how happy I am to have won this cup. I have never worked harder or suffered more than in trying to get it. It has been said that I enjoyed the Tolley match, but, much as I love Cyril, I would not have been glad to see him in the next round. (Laughter.) I have said before that St. Andrews has been a little bit too good to me when I was lucky enough to win the Open here, but I want to say now that it has made me feel happier than the winning of any other cup in the past."*

Jones left St. Andrews for Paris, where he vacationed with his wife for a week. Then he went to England, where he won the Open Championship with a record-breaking score at Hoylake. Following a ticker-tape parade in New York, Jones finished out the season with victories in the U.S. Open and U.S. Amateur. Having achieved his lofty goal - later named the Grand Slam - the 28-year-old Jones retired from competition.

1936

INFORMAL VISIT

In 1936, the Olympic Games were held in Berlin and Jones' friend from Georgia, hurdler Forrest "Spec" Towns, was favored to win a gold medal. Jones and a few friends agreed that the event would serve as a *"splendid excuse for playing golf in Britain,"* and the trip was soon arranged.

The contingent arrived in London, played Sunningdale and then headed north to Gleneagles in Scotland. Jones then decided a pilgrimage to St. Andrews was in order. *"I could not leave here without playing at St. Andrews,"* he said.

A chauffeur was dispatched to St. Andrews to place four names in the ballot for a tee time at the Old Course: *F. Hodgson, D. Garlington, E. Kelley, and R.T. Jones Jr.*

The party traveled to St. Andrews in the morning and had lunch at the R & A clubhouse. Looking out a window, they noticed several thousand townspeople assembled down the length of the first fairway. Jones concluded that he had the misfortune of attempting to play a private match during an important championship. Little did he know that the news of his coming had spread rapidly throughout the town. Businesses closed their doors as the locals eagerly awaited their hero.

The scheduled match was spontaneously revised and after a few holes, only Jones and Willie Auchterlonie, the R & A's honorary professional, continued to play. The gallery had swelled to 4,000.

Jones rose to the occasion. He later described the day as the *"best golf I had played for four years and certainly never since."* At the sixth he was faced with a choice of the old St. Andrews run-up shot or a fancy pitch. Jones said to himself, *"Look Jones, these people are all expecting you to play that run-up, so don't you funk it."* The ball rolled up to the green and finished six feet from the flag. Jones holed it for a 3. Inspired by the *"hometown crowd,"* Jones made 2 at the par-3 eighth and turned in 32. Perhaps it was poetic justice that Jones and *"Old Man Par"* each acquitted themselves with dignity on that day as Jones was round in 71 or 72 - depending on which account you read.

Jones later spoke of the event: *"I shall never forget that round. It was not anything like a serious golf match, but it was a wonderful experience. There was sort of a holiday mood in the crowd. It seemed, or they made it appear at least, that they were just glad to see me back, and however I played golf was all right with them, only they wanted to see it."*

1958

WORLD AMATEUR

TEAM CHAMPIONSHIP AND FREEMASON CEREMONY

Bobby Jones dreamed of a return to Britain after 1936, but never gave it serious consideration until the inaugural World Amateur Team Championship was scheduled for St. Andrews. Jones accepted the duty of captain for the American team and for the first time traveled by airplane across the Atlantic. By this time his affliction with syringeomyelia, a debilitating neurological disease, had long ended his days as a golfer.

Walking with the aid of two canes toward Rusack's Hotel, Jones commented, *"It's been a long time getting back - 22 years. But it's worth waiting for."* With the Scottish twilight shining on the links, Jones quipped, *"I'm going to get in my electric buggy and travel all over the Old Course. It will be the first buggy ever to go round there and I bet you it'll be the last."* Jones' words were never so accurate, as no buggies (motorized golf carts) are permitted to this day on the Old Course.

In this contest, the Americans fought a hard battle, but the Australian team prevailed to win the Eisenhower Cup.

But it was not on the links where Jones would shine on this trip. The Younger Graduation Hall of St. Andrews University on the evening of October 9, 1958, was the venue for what Jones called the *"most impressive and emotional experience"* in his life.

The town clerk had cabled Jones a month before inquiring if he would accept the honor of being a *"Freeman of St. Andrews."* Jones accepted, but did not really consider the matter to be more significant than receiving the perfunctory key to the city, of which he already had a key ring full.

Upon arriving at St. Andrews, Jones was given a short history of the honor, including the fact that he would

126

be the second American - Benjamin Franklin being the first in 1759 - to receive such an honor. The benefits were tantamount to nothing less than citizenship with the traditional rights to hunt rabbits, dig divots, and even bleach his laundry on the first and 18th fairways near the Swilken Burn.

Jones met the town clerk's request for an advance copy of his speech with a nervous reply that he was still working on it. Jones did prepare essential notes, but he would trust his natural instincts of carefully weighing the circumstances and measuring his reply on the spot ex tempore.

Seventeen-hundred people filled Younger Hall to capacity on the appointed evening. Some of those waiting outside would write letters to the editor of the St. Andrews Citizen complaining that another thousand people should have been anticipated for this singular historical event.

The town clerk, adorned in white wig and crimson robe, opened the ceremony with a prayer and reading of the citation. Then, Provost Robert Leonard, resplendent in an ermine-trimmed robe adorned with the chains of office, rose to speak about St. Andrews' newest citizen. The short history of Jones' initial misunderstanding and dislike of the Old Course in 1921 was embellished by the subsequent spawning of a love affair unequaled in give and take between the champion and the people. Leonard remarked, *"As representatives of St. Andrews, we wish to honor Mr. Jones because we feel drawn to him by ties of affection and personal regard of a particularly cordial nature, and because we know that he himself has declared his own enduring affection for the place and for its people."*

Jones was then invited to sign the Burgess Roll, followed by presentation of a beautifully engraved silver casket with the scroll conferring the Freedom honor. Jones whispered that he did not desire any assistance in rising from his chair and awkwardly shuffled to the podium. He positioned himself and began to weave a theme of friendship and admiration that, at times, compelled him to pause lest he be so overcome with emotion that he couldn't continue. *"I just want to say to you that this is the finest thing that has ever happened to me."* Jones reminisced about his impetuous withdrawal from the 1921 Open at the *"ripe old age of 19 years"* and admitted that he didn't know much about golf then. However, after talking to a lot of transplanted Scots and much studying, Jones admitted he never lost another contest on the Old Course. He recalled the miniature British Amateur trophy sent following the Grand Slam and treasured his visit in 1936 when the townspeople locked their stores and walked the fairways while witnessing the best golf he had played in years.

Jones concluded his speech with the memorable observation, *"I could take out of my life everything except my experiences at St. Andrews and I would still have a rich and full life."* At the end of his remarks, the audience stood and regaled him with *"For He's a Jolly Good Fellow"* and *"Will Ye No' Come Back Again?"* Jones then amazed everyone by walking unassisted to his electric cart and leaving the hall. Henry Longhurst observed that it was several minutes before anyone could speak in a calm voice.

GAME CALLED: DARKNESS

On December 18, 1971, golfers on the Old Course stopped their play as the flag on the R & A clubhouse was lowered to half-staff. News had been received that Bobby Jones had died.

A memorial service was held in St. Andrews on May 4, 1972, at the Holy Trinity Church. A touching tribute was delivered by Roger Wethered, who first competed against Jones 50 years earlier in the 1922 Walker Cup. Following the service, there was a procession of dignitaries through the streets, led by a hall porter carrying one of the R & A's ceremonial silver clubs. Even to this day the memory of Bobby Jones' march on Britain is kindled in the hearts of these people.

Chapter 7
The Impregnable Quadrilateral: The Grand Slam

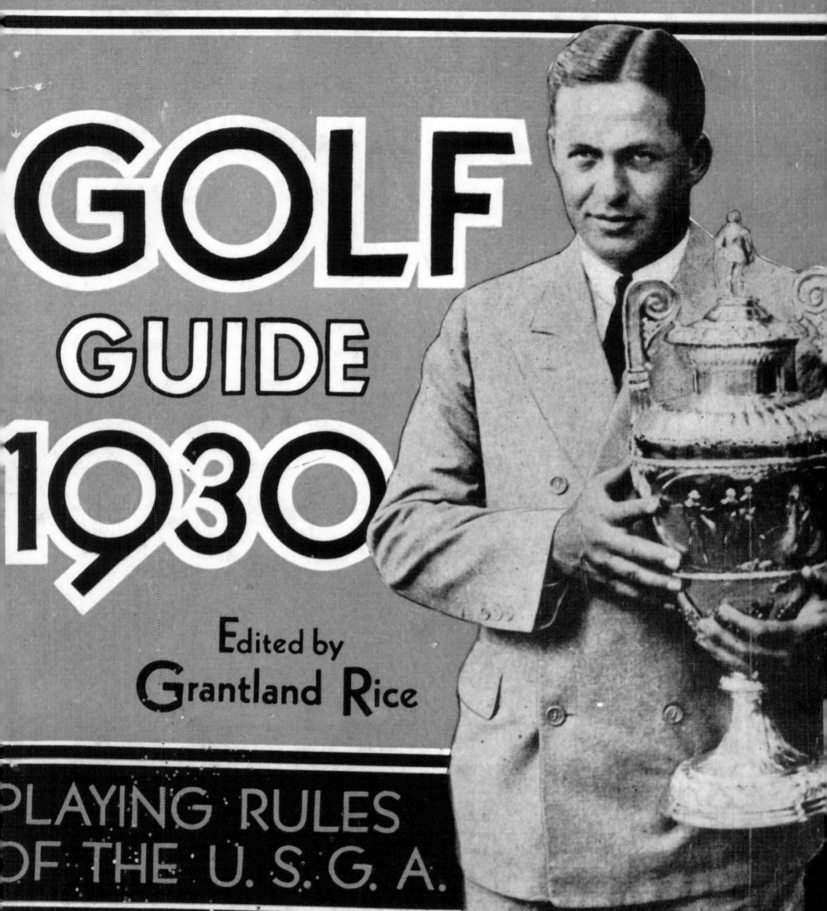

NO. 3x • PRICE 35 CENTS

SPALDING'S
ATHLETIC LIBRARY

GOLF GUIDE 1930

Edited by Grantland Rice

PLAYING RULES OF THE U.S.G.A.

American Sports Publishing Company

45 Rose St. New York

Captain of the English team, Roger Wethered, congratulates Bobby Jones, captain of the American Walker Cup team, after the American team had defeated their British rivals and retained possession of the Walker Cup in May 1930. Wethered once commented:

In point of physique, Bobby Jones is noticeably far stronger than the ordinary golfer. The mere ceremony of shaking hands with him provides a faint clue to his actual strength. By this I do not insinuate that he shakes hands otherwise than very reasonably. But one unconsciously realizes in the action a latent force that is significant; beneath the surface there lurks a grip of iron and wrist as flexible as steel which partly explains the sting which he applies so effortlessly to the ball.

"The Amateur Championship at St. Andrews was won by the right man, Bobby Jones, but it was a desperately close run thing," noted Bernard Darwin. Jones is driving from the sixth tee in his opening match against Syd Roper, an ex-coalminer from Nottingham. Roper stands behind Jones waiting to drive. At this point in the match, Jones was 5-under par but only 3 up on Roper. In the end, Jones prevailed by 3 to 2, but only after Roper scored 15 4s and a single 5. Jones acknowledged that Roper's keen play would have demolished anyone else in the field.

The most talked about shot in the Jones-Roper match occurred on the 427-yard par 4 fourth hole. Jones' drive rolled 300 yards from the tee into the Cottage Bunker and resting about 150 yards from the flag. From that lie, Bob struck the ball with a spade mashie and it *"descended lightly, just beyond a little rise at the front of the green; the spin took hold promptly, and instead of bounding the ball rolled and seemed to slide over the glassy surface, slower and slower, and at last trickled into the hole without touching the flagstaff."* Roper's brave response was to halve the next hole with a birdie 4. During the hysteria which greeted the shot, Keeler overheard one spectator comment, *"Too bad he was in a bunker."*

In the fourth round, Jones met the defending champion, Cyril Tolley. Jones wrote, *"Tolley was one of those players who had a flair for the spectacular. Although he did it in a different way, he played the game, like Hagen, in the grand manner."* Every man, woman, and child at St. Andrews went out to see the match.

Tolley, perhaps the longest driver of the ball in all of the United Kingdom, at the finish of a prodigious drive from the second tee. The drama was prolonged through the 17th Road Hole as the match was all square. Tolley's third shot was a deft pitch over the Road Bunker and was *"bravely judged so that it trembled momentarily on the edge of the bunker before trickling down a foot from the hole."* It was Jones' conviction that Tolley's shot:

"has never been surpassed for exquisitely beautiful execution. I shall carry to my grave the impression of the lovely little stroke with which he dropped the ball so softly in exactly the right spot, so that in the only possible way it finished dead to the hole. Tolley himself, after the passage of twenty-eight years, confirmed to me that this was the finest shot of his life. I am sure that it was."

Jones negotiates the Swilken Burn crossing the first and 18th fairways at the Old Course. Tolley was not so successful in jumping over the stymie laid by Jones on the first playoff hole after they finished all square at the 18th. Although Jones regretted that the match ended with a stymie, nevertheless, he decried the abolishment of the stymie:

With the stymie in the game, match-play golf becomes an exciting duel in which the player must always be on guard against a sudden, often demoralizing thrust. More than anything else, it points up the value of always being the closer to the hole on the shot to the green and after the first putt. The player who can maintain the upper hand in the play up to the hole rarely suffers from a stymie. In my observation, the stymie has more often been the means of enforcing a decision in favor of the deserving player rather than the contrary. I think it merits a respected place in the game. I know a return to it would greatly enhance the interest and excitement of match-play golf for player and spectator alike.

Bobby Jones is escorted back to the clubhouse after he had been surrounded by the enthusiastic crowd following his match with Tolley. The constables are justly proud of their "collar."

Francis Ouimet wrote of playing against Jones:

"I can only describe a match against Bobby in this manner: It is just as though you got your hand caught in a buzz saw. He coasts along serenely waiting for you to miss a shot, and the moment you do, he has you on the hook and you never get off. If the young man were human, he would make a mistake once in a while, but he never makes any mistakes. He manages to do everything better than anybody else. He can drive straighter than any man living. He is perfectly machinelike in his iron play, and on the greens he is a demon. If you can beat that type of man, I should like the recipe. But he is more than a great golfer. He is a grand competitor."

As Jones emerged victorious from each fiercely contested match, O.B. Keeler became persuaded that a Jones victory was simply *"in the book."* Keeler explained:

The story of the 1930 British Championship seems to me to confirm, or at any rate, strongly to support a sort of hypothesis that had been forming in the back of my head for years — that golf tournaments are matters of destiny, and that the result is all in the book before a shot is hit. Looking back over Bobby's eight matches, you may see crisis after crisis in those furious encounters with Tolley, Johnston and Voigt where the least slip in nerve or skill or plain fortune would have brought defeat to Bobby's dearest ambition. Yet at every crisis he stood up to the shot with something I can define only as inevitability and performed what was needed with all the certainty of a natural phenomenon.

Bobby Jones drives from the first tee on the Old Course at St. Andrews. Bob said:

In my humble opinion, St. Andrews is the most fascinating golf course I have ever played...To account for the fascination of the place to one who has not seen it is a very difficult matter...There is always a way at St. Andrews, although it is not always the obvious way, and in trying to find it, there is more to be learned on this English course than in playing a hundred ordinary American golf courses.

Bob Jones' march into the final match with Roger Wethered was met with mixed reviews. Sir James Lieshman, a Scotsman, remarked, *"His luck is as fixed as the orbit of a planet. He cannot be beaten here."* Another spectator in the gallery quipped, *"They ought to burn him at the stake. He's a witch."* As he had done during the Walker Cup matches, Jones defeated Wethered 7 and 6 in the finals.

Although Mr. Jones was from the other side of the Atlantic, Skene said, St. Andrews could *"claim a bit of him as he was a member of the Royal & Ancient Club."* Some members of the Royal & Ancient Club later sent Bob a silver miniature replica of the British Open Championship trophy with old Tom Morris' likeness on top with the inscription: *"To a golfer matchless in skill and chivalrous in spirit."*

This photo made immediately after the final match of the British Amateur Championship was rushed to London and radioed to New York. It was the most revolutionary technology then known. Today we casually refer to this as a facsimile (fax).

Mid-Week Pictorial

"A National Magazine of News Pictures"

VOL. XXXI, No. 18.   NEW YORK, WEEK ENDING JUNE 21, 1930.   PRICE TEN CENTS

The One Cup He Needed to Make His Collection Complete

Bobby Jones of Atlanta, Who Had Won Every Other Golfing Trophy Worth the Having, at Last Grasps the Emblem of Supremacy in the British Amateur Championship by His Defeat of Roger Wethered at St. Andrews.

(Times Wide World Photos.)

After winning his first British Amateur, O.B. Keeler asked Jones, *"Will this victory inspire you with renewed enthusiasm and determination at Hoylake?"* Jones demurred: *"Quite the contrary. I've won the British Amateur — at last. My little expedition is a success, no matter what happens at Hoylake. And I'm going to relax a bit. Mary and I are going over to Paris."* Although Jones downplayed the significance of his second British Championship at Hoylake, privately he knew that it was crucial to achieving the Grand Slam, which was his plan all along:

The inescapable fact was that I could not win all four without the first one, and this first one had always been for me the most difficult. This one tournament had put me more than one-quarter of the distance on the way to my goal and, in effect, might be said to have put a price support under my crop.

This photo shows Bob during the qualifying rounds when even noted London golfwriter Bob Howard recognized that Jones had a *"fifth gear"* not possessed by his competitors:

Bobby Jones took a turn among the ordinary mortals by compiling a score of 77. It was plenty good enough for qualifying purposes. But although he said he was very dissatisfied with his golf, I am quite sure he could have done considerably better if the need had existed.

144

Bob's first three rounds were 70, 72, 74, which were forged through *"stolid patience, and the tempered philosophy gained from years of defeat and seasons of disappointment, over every kind of championship golf course and against every type of field the game affords."* Cyril Tolley once observed about Jones:

I believe he is really a score player, and although a magnificent match-player, he is gifted with one very unfortunate peculiarity. That is, he generally makes his opponent play better than he has ever played before.

Indeed, Archie Compston took the third round lead with a masterful 68.

The modest smile of a tired and happy 1930 British Open champion.

Few people realize that Jones played golf under a very curious handicap. Nobody hated him, outside of the few who were jealous of his success and his bearing. He was probably one of the best loved athletes who ever went into competition. Every step that he took on a golf course from the time he first came to fame, back in 1923, was dogged by worshipping and well meaning friends who played every stroke with him, moaned and sympathized when he went into traps or trouble, cheered every success, and clung to him as though he was their prophet. Well, he was, too. It must be remembered that he was a living example and proof that this very cranky and cantankerous game can be played.

New York's second tickertape parade for Bobby Jones was in 1930. He is still the only person to ever enjoy two such honors. (Lindbergh, Eisenhower, Ben Hogan, to name a few, had only one.)

Veteran sportswriter Paul Gallico wrote:

I am, by nature, a hero-worshiper, as, I guess, most of us are, but in all the years of contact with the famous ones of sport, I have found only one that would stand up in every way as a gentleman as well as a celebrity, a fine, decent, human being as well as a newsprint personage, and who never once, since I have known him, has let me down in my estimate of him. That one is Robert Tyre Jones, Jr., the golf player from Atlanta, Georgia... In Scotland and England, where he played in tournaments, the natives practically made a god out of him. He remained unaffected. He was exposed to the attacks of the most ill-bred and ruthless pests in the world, the curiosity seeking golf nuts and autograph hunters and his privacy was assailed from morning until night. He never in all his career could engage in a friendly golf match (except on his home course) without being followed and swamped with attention and more often, annoyance. Yet, I never heard of his being deliberately rude. The only thing I think he ever permitted himself to do when chivvied and harassed beyond human endurance, particularly during an important tournament, was quietly to turn and walk away.

Jones:

"had a sense of proportion uncommon in a man with a vigorously perfectionist side to his nature... He had incredible strength of character. As a young man, he was able to stand up to just about the best that life can offer, which is not easy, and later he stood up with equal grace to just about the worst. On top of everything else, he had tremendous personal magnetism... Everybody adored him — not just dyed-in-the-wool golfers, but people who had never struck a golf ball or had the least desire to. They admired the ingrained modesty, the humor, and the generosity of spirit that were evident in Jones' remarks and deportment. They liked the way he looked, this handsome, clean cut young man, whose eyes gleamed with both a frank boyishness and a perceptiveness far beyond his years... Jones, in short, was the model American athlete come to life, and it is to the credit of the American public that they recognized this almost instantly," wrote Herbert Warren Wind.

In the 1930 US Open Championship at Interlachen CC Bob played a famous stroke of luck in the second round known as the *"Lily Pad Shot."* Bob pushed his tee shot on the ninth hole on the right bank of the lake, thus requiring a hard spoon shot to reach the green in two strokes. Jones decided to go for the green, as he had done in several previous rounds, and took his usual drowsy backswing with his spoon. As he reached the top of the backswing, two young girls broke and ran as if to cross the fairway up ahead. In his peripheral vision, Jones saw this, flinched and half topped the ball which *"struck the water twenty yards from the farther bank, skipped like a flat stone once and again, and hopped out on the smooth slope, thirty yards short of the green."* Spectators swore that the ball had hit a lily pad floating in the lake and, but for the luck of the Irish, the ball should have been resting at the bottom of the lake *"along with Davey Jones' locker."*

After the *"Lily Pad Shot,"* Jones capitalized on his good fortune by hitting a wee pitch two feet from the flag and sinking a birdie 4, which helped to put him in second place at the midway point of the championship.

Bobby Jones, making a short putt during the final day's play at Interlachen. *"The remarkable thing about this championship is just this,"* Hagen told Grantland Rice. *"Here is the greatest field ever assembled on any golf course. Here you have the survivors of 1200 entries and yet it is one field against one man — Bobby Jones. Nothing like this has ever happened in golf, from the days of Vardon and Taylor and Braid to the present moment. It is almost unbelievable, but it is true."*

On the final hole, Bob left his approach 40 feet below the small plateau where the hole was cut. Every muscle in Jones' body quivered as he stroked the ball in an effort only to get it close enough for a tap in. Miraculously, the 40-foot putt went down for a birdie 3 and a 2-stroke victory for his third leg of the Grand Slam.

Jones receiving congratulations after play at Interlachen. Bob would have to wait an hour and see if MacDonald Smith could make a 3 on the last hole to tie him. Smith made par (in a round of 70) and although he had cut 5 strokes away from Jones' lead, he still finished 2 behind.

Bobby Jones and his 1930 U.S. Open caddie. On his victory at Interlachen, O.B. Keeler wrote, *"I do not think he needs to add anything more to his record in the Open Championships. He may live to be a very old man, but he will never live to see anyone else match his record of the last eight years in the United States Open: four first places and three second places, two of them after a tie and a play off."* [On June 15, 1980, Jack Nicklaus won the U.S. Open for the fourth time with a record 272 at Baltusrol; he also finished second four times in 1960, 1968, 1971 and 1982.] On the issue of comparisons of great players to his record, Jones remarked:

"I think we must agree that all a man can do is beat the people who are around at the same time he is. He cannot win from those who came before any more than he can from those who may come afterward. It is grossly unfair to anyone who takes pride in the record he is able to compile that he must see it compared to those of other players who have been competing against entirely different people under wholly different conditions."

U.S.G.A. President Findlay Douglas presents Bobby Jones his fourth U.S. Open Championship trophy. *"If you enter a tournament, and don't cheat, and happen to make the lowest score, they have to give you the cup."*

"Double Runner-Up" MacDonald Smith enjoys a moment with the 1930 U.S. Open champion, Bobby Jones. Smith was twice runner up to Jones during the Grand Slam, both at Hoylake and Interlachen. He is one of the greatest players never to win a major championship.

Bobby Jones arrived at Philadelphia's Broad Street Station at 8:50 a.m. on September 17, 1930 to prepare for the 1930 National Amateur Golf Championship at the Merion Cricket Club - the fourth leg of the Grand Slam. In an upstairs room of the Interlachen CC clubhouse, Bob decided that no matter what happened at Merion, he was finished with competitive golf. He did not, however, tell the press at that time. Instead, when asked *"what are you going to do when you retire?"* Jones said, *"You'd better tell them O.B., you know."* Having just emerged in the shower and wrapped in a towel, Keeler stepped up on a bench and recited:

If ever I become a rich man, or if ever I grow to be old, I will build a house with a deep thatch to shelter me from the cold, I will hold my house in the high woods within a walk of the sea, and the men that were boys when I was a boy shall sit and drink with me.

The crowd surrounding the scoreboard at Merion knew that it was *"Jones Against The Field."* Even though the championship was played at the height of the depression, the total paid attendance at Merion was 35,450 people who paid $55,319. (In 1964, total receipts at the U.S. Open were only $17,261). Francis Powers of the Chicago News analogized the scene to Grantland Rice's description of the Four Horsemen of the Notre Dame football team:

There goes another race by the Four Horsemen of the Apocalypse over the fairways of Merion, and this time their names are Jones, Jones, Jones, and Jones.

O.B. Keeler employed another analogy of the Merion event:

The premier golfing firm of all the world, Jones, Jones, Jones, and Jones. Succeeding ages may match it if they can.

Regarding the crowds, Jones said, *"I do not have anything against the human race as a tribe, but I prefer them in small doses."* Gene Sarazen especially noticed Jones' reaction to crowds:

Jones was always polite toward his idolatrous galleries, but I think he regarded them as an element that could deter his concentration if he let it invade his thoughts...At the same time, in a unique and wondrous way, Bob quietly unleashed the most furious concentration of any golfer, in those days when it was Jones versus the field. This arduous dedication to the job at hand left him spent and weary after each round. Bob never hung around the locker room long after the day's play was over.

Bobby Jones marching to victory during the 1930 U.S. Amateur Championship at Merion. A detachment of 50 Marines was on hand at Merion, mainly to guard Bob Jones and help control the galleries. Bob's caddy, 19-year-old Howard Rexford, and Chick Ridley are walking to Bob's left. The Marines helped clear the way for Jones' fast pace of play. It took only two hours 10 minutes for Jones to dispatch his first-round opponent, C. Ross (Sandy) Somerville, of Canada. (An average of 9.3 minutes per hole or two hours 48 minutes for 18 holes.) *Golf is not a funeral though both can be sad things,"* Bernard Darwin wrote.

Jones expressed his contempt for slow play by describing an anecdote in his law practice. A lawyer went to extraordinary lengths to defend his client who was thereafter convicted anyway. The trial had been long drawn out, lasting nearly a month, and the lawyer had made quite a lot of noise and stormed eloquently in his argument. Meeting a brother lawyer on the street a few days later the case came up in discussion, and the lawyer asked his friend what he thought of his conduct of the trial. His friend replied:

Well, I think you could have reached the same result with a whole lot less effort.

159

Bobby Jones' final putt on the 11th hole to win the Grand Slam. The margin of victory was 8 and 7. After Jones' ball went dead to the hole, his caddy, Howard Rexford, retrieved Jones' Spalding Black Dot ball. He kept it for 30 years until using it in an afternoon match at his Philadelphia golf club where he lost it. Most of the 18,000 spectators stormed the green, and the players sought refuge behind the Marines. Jones' walk back to the clubhouse was described by *New York Times* writer William Richardson as *"the most triumphant journey that any man ever travelled in sport."*

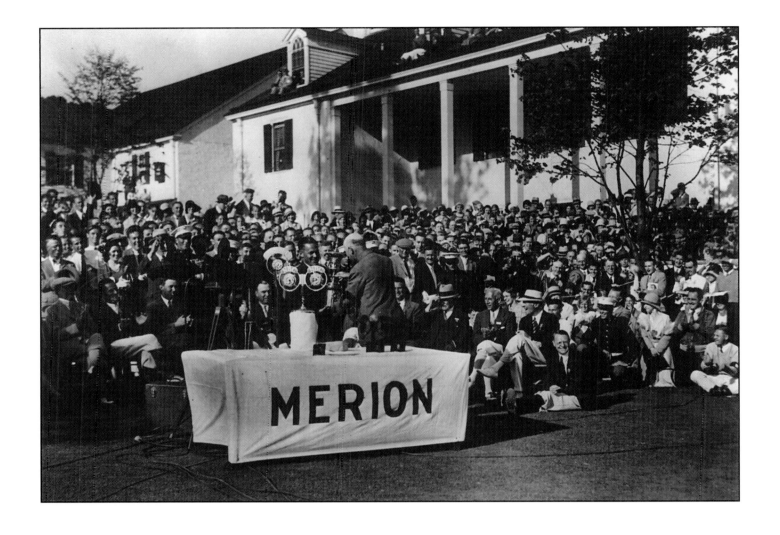

Bobby Jones is presented his fifth U.S. Amateur Championship trophy by USGA President Findlay Douglas.

Bobby Jones with the four Grand Slam championship trophies.

I have said it before, and I don't mind repeating it. I'm glad, mighty glad to be back home. That's the best part of these things; after they are over you can come back home. And I'm going to be mighty hard to get out of town again.

Reporters struggled with superlative after superlative to describe the heights to which Jones had ascended. *Atlanta Journal's* O.B. Keeler dubbed it the *"Grand Slam"* borrowing a bridge term. George Trevor of the *New York Sun* wrote that Jones had *"stormed the impregnable quadrilateral of golf."* Embellishing on that term, Keeler added:

This victory, the fourth major title in the same season and in the space of four months, had now and for all time entrenched Bobby Jones safely within the "Impregnable Quadrilateral of Golf", that granite fortress that he alone could take by escalade, and that others may attack in vain, forever.

Chapter 8
Portrait of a Gentleman

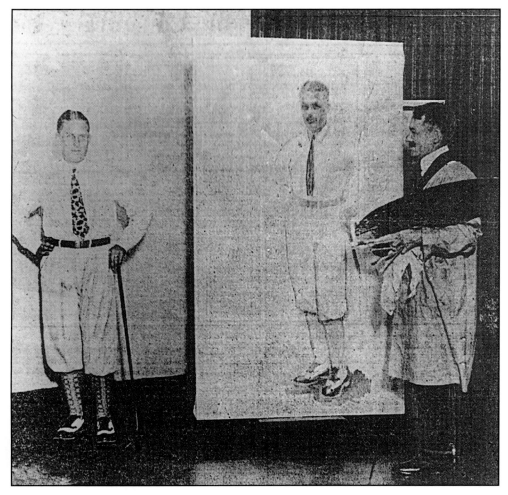

When Bob Jones won "The Double," a group of prominent Atlantans commissioned portrait artist Wayman Adams (1883-1959) to paint the champion. Adams was a leading portrait painter in America and considered portraits of presidents Harding, Coolidge, and Hoover among his best work. Observers marvelled at the magic of his paint-loaded brush and masterful exhibition of the alla-prima technique. Especially when working on a life-sized canvas, Adams struck a pose not unlike that of a sword fighter attacking the canvas with movements of thrust and parry.

One of the members of the Atlanta committee which commissioned the painting, J.J. Haverty, wrote Adams on August 19, 1926 with the following ideas that might be incorporated into the portrait:

I wish to respectfully suggest further, that in composing the portrait certain things appropriate to the person and conditions should be considered. First — Bobby Jones is not a sport, but a sportsman. He is not in the category of the prize fighter or other athletes whose reputations depend upon their physical skill or animal instincts, and who, like the Mule, have no "pride of ancestry nor hope of posterity." Bobby Jones' victories in golf are not the result of special physical conditions or accomplishments, but are due to a high order of mental capacity, concentration and self-control, supported by youthful enthusiasm, great determination, superb ambition, and modesty of demeanor. His life work is not that of a golf player. His mental qualifications and inclinations direct him to the law, and he will enter college next month to study law, with the intention of making it his life work. Golf hereafter with him will be only a plaything, and yet today he is the greatest golfer in the world, because of his antecedents, his blood, and his youthful, praiseworthy ambition.

Success has not spoiled him; he is as modest today and as unassuming as he was when a boy of twelve. His future may mean a political career, and I submit that his portrait should be composed with the thought in mind that you are not making a portrait of a sport, but of a young man with a high order of mental capacity, of wonderful concentration, self-control, culture, determination, and ambition. Then you will have a portrait that will do justice to him and to you — that will in no sense suggest a funny picture or a caricature of the man or the land in which he lives.

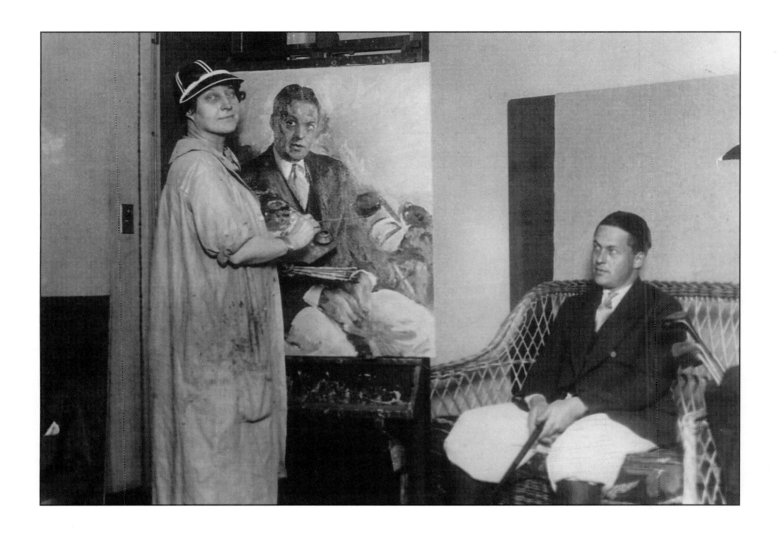

Bob was the subject of a portrait by Boston artist Margaret Fitzhugh Browne (1884-1972) in 1928. Browne also painted Spanish King Alphonso XIII for the New York Yacht Club and Henry Ford. In her paintings, Browne usually accompanied her sitters with some telling attribute helping to identify the subject. Her interpretation of Bob Jones included a bag of hickory-shafted golf clubs resting gently on the edge of the bench upon which Bob sat. The handle of one club rests casually in his hands. The portrait was featured in the High Museum of Art in Atlanta. Mrs. Browne also painted Atlanta Athletic Club President Scott Hudson reposed at the Atlanta Athletic Club.

After Bob's victory in the British Open at Royal Liverpool in Hoylake, artist J.A.A. Berrie captured Jones' likeness on June 15, 1930. Sir Ernest Royden commissioned the painting and presented it to the Wallasey Golf Club located only a few miles from Royal Liverpool. Bob explained the manner in which the painting was created:

Mr. Berrie kept me occupied for not more than 30 minutes and during that time pleasantly refreshed me with a whiskey and soda. As an object lesson in painless portraiture, this was the best I have ever seen.

After Berrie had captured Bob's countenance, he left the studio, but not before taking off his blue sweater and giving it to a member of the Wallasey Golf Club who put it on and finished sitting for the remainder of the painting from roughly the neck down. The painting was signed and dated by Jones before he left.

Berrie painted various copies of his first effort which altered the pose, clothing, and backgrounds. These later examples are reposed at Royal Liverpool, Royal Lytham and St. Annes, Sunningdale, Augusta National, and the Atlanta History Center.

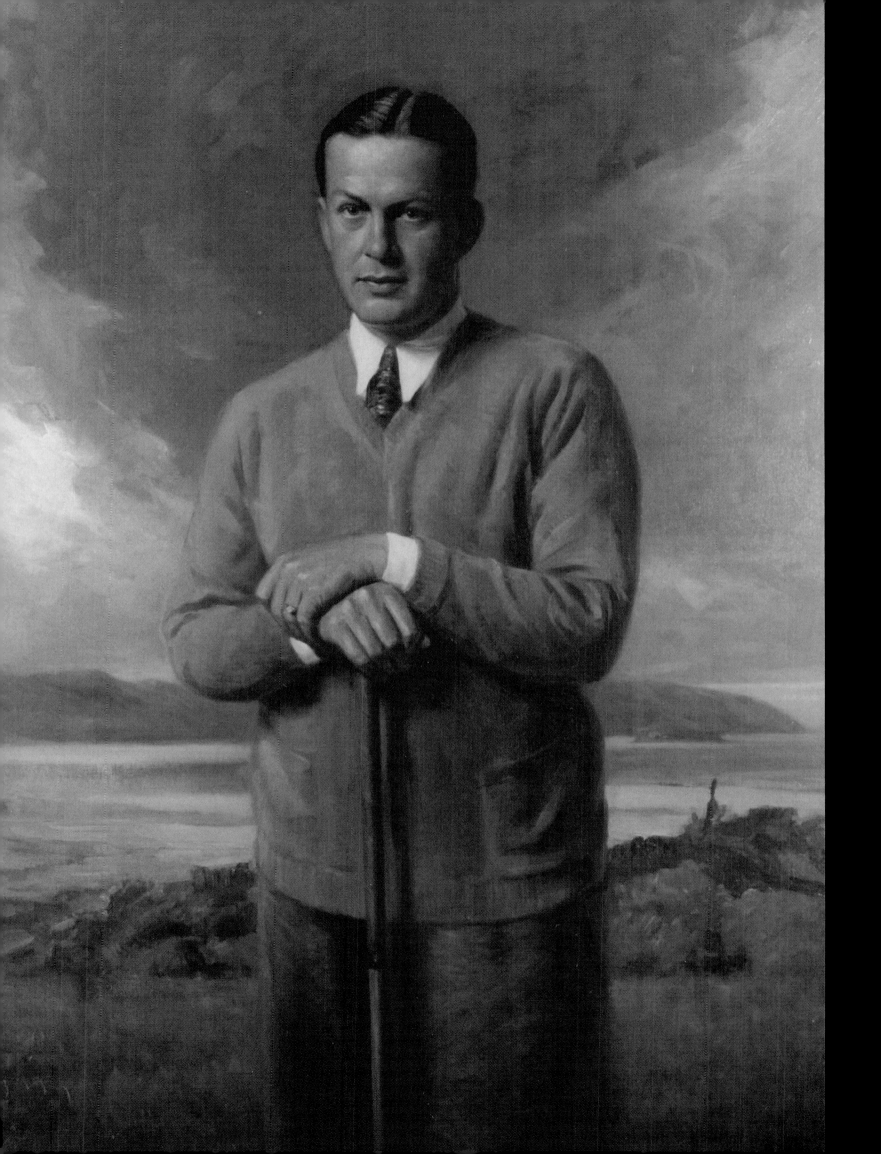

O.B. Keeler's favorite photograph of Bob Jones was this one taken on Bob's *"last look"* at the hole before commencing his stroke. From this photograph, artist William Steene painted Bob's portrait shown on the opposite page. Steene was born in Syracuse, New York, (1888) and studied at the National Academy of Design, the Art Students League of New York Chase Beaux Arts, Calarossi, and Julian's in Paris. All the details, such as skin tones, grip, and clothing, were painted from actual life. The portrait was exhibited in the Grand Central Gallery in New York and hung for years in John Jarrell, Inc. in Atlanta.

FIFTEEN CENTS

September 22, 1930

TIME

The Weekly Newsmagazine

ROBERT TYRE JONES JR.

His only peer was Percy.

(See SPORT)

Volume XVI

Number 12

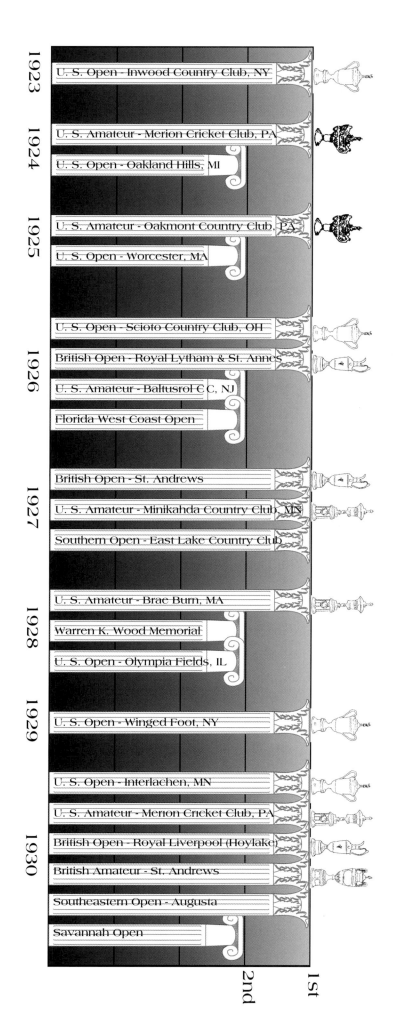

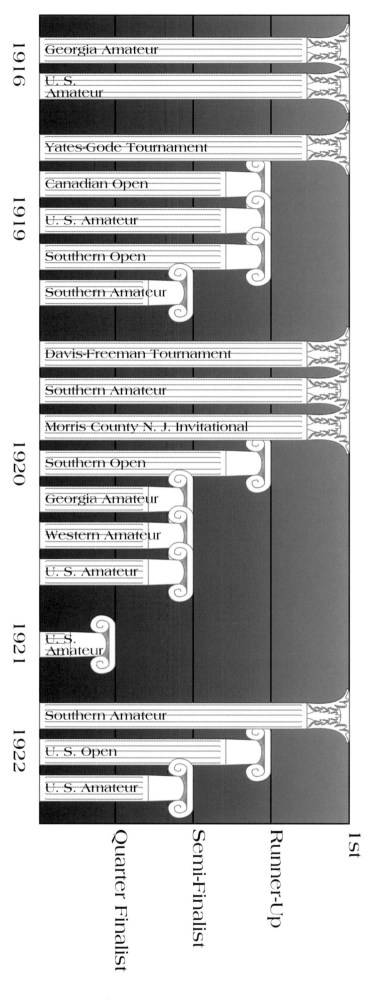

Georgia Amateur

U. S. Amateur

Yates-Gode Tournament

Canadian Open

U. S. Amateur

Southern Open

Southern Amateur

Davis-Freeman Tournament

Southern Amateur

Morris County N. J. Invitational

Southern Open

Georgia Amateur

Western Amateur

U. S. Amateur

U. S. Amateur

Southern Amateur

U. S. Open

U. S. Amateur

1916

1919

1920

1921

1922

Quarter Finalist

Semi-Finalist

Runner-Up

1st

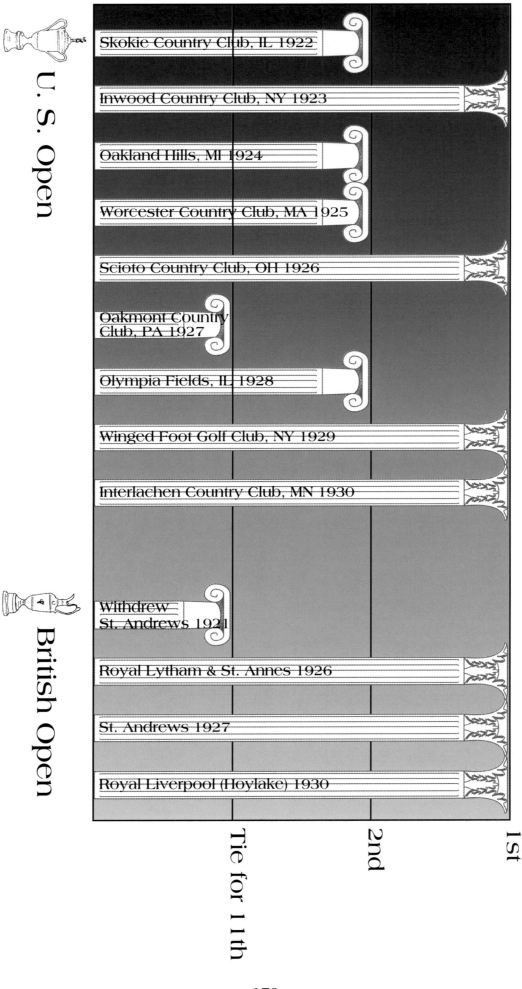

Bobby Jones placed first or second in 11 of 13 Open Championships

U. S. Open

Skokie Country Club, IL 1922
Inwood Country Club, NY 1923
Oakland Hills, MI 1924
Worcester Country Club, MA 1925
Scioto Country Club, OH 1926
Oakmont Country Club, PA 1927
Olympia Fields, IL 1928
Winged Foot Golf Club, NY 1929
Interlachen Country Club, MN 1930

British Open

Withdrew St. Andrews 1921
Royal Lytham & St. Annes 1926
St. Andrews 1927
Royal Liverpool (Hoylake) 1930

1st
2nd
Tie for 11th

For 37 years, Bob Jones kept his silver and gold medals won in competition in a small chest in his Tuxedo Road estate. On July 19, 1967, Jones offered the collection to the United States Golf Association Museum, of which Jones was a committee member. On July 25, 1967, USGA President Ward Foshay enthusiastically accepted the generous gift and promised the medals would be the "CROWN JEWELS" of the Golf House Museum. The USGA kindly permitted these photographs to be taken and displayed here.

BOB JONES' PROUDEST ACCOMPLISHMENT
First or Second Place finish in 11 of 13 British and American Open Championships.

Regarding the first medal won in 1923 Jones remembered: *"Do you know, it's hard as the devil to get one of those things!"*

THE GRAND SLAM MEDALS
AND WALKER CUP BALL

AAU SULLIVAN AWARD: "THE BLACK SHEEP AWARD" The Amateur Athletic Union presented the James E. Sullivan Award to Bob Jones in 1930 commemorating the nation's outstanding amateur athlete. Jones never kept the medal among his others and laughed to his secretary Jean Marshall Splawn, *"Take it down to Shoney's and see of you can get a $1.75 hamburger for it."* The medal was appraised by two jewelers in 1967, and the *"black sheep award"* was determined to contain a gold value of $10,000.

In 1954, Thomas Stevens was again commissioned to paint Bob at the finish of a full swing (opposite, top). The portrait hangs in the Bob Jones' room at the U.S.G.A. Golf House in Far Hills, New Jersey. Later, President Eisenhower copied the painting (opposite, bottom), and the painting was hung in the Bob Jones' cabin at Augusta National Golf Club. President Eisenhower was never quite happy with the way Bob's eyes turned out and points to them in the above photograph.

Lt. Col. Robert T. Jones, Jr., was photographed by J. Hixson Kinsella in his war togs worn while overseas. On March 23, 1945, the photograph won a perfect score and first prize in the Atlanta Camera Club monthly contest. It was only the second picture in the organization's history to win a perfect score. Using this photograph, University of Georgia sociology professor Bo Williams painted Bob's portrait (opposite page). An amateur artist, Professor Williams painted other members of his family and miscellaneous friends. He was self-taught by using his daughter, Peggy's, paints after she got married and went to South America. The painting was presented by Morton Hodgson to the Highlands Country Club.

Bob is shown wearing the club jacket of the Augusta National Golf Club (ANGC).

Courtesy East Lake Country Club

Courtesy Atlanta Athletic Club

187

On April 6, 1959, Bob Jones graced the cover of Sports Illustrated holding his legendary putter, Calamity Jane, and wearing his green Master's coat. In the background is the Augusta National Golf Club. The painting was completed by Aaron Shikler, and is reposed at Augusta National.

During a rainstorm on Lake Sinclair, Bob Jones and Charlie Elliott pulled underneath a bridge to seek shelter. Bob became amused when Charlie couldn't quite get his camera to operate. This is the final result of Charlie's efforts to capture Bob after a colorful quip about the incident.

During Shell's "Wonderful World of Golf" series, host Gene Sarazen interviewed Bob Jones at Peachtree Golf Club in Atlanta. The match between Sam Snead and Julius Boros was aired on February 25, 1967.

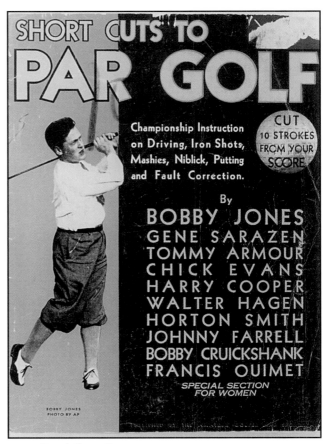

Magazines With Bob Jones On The Cover.

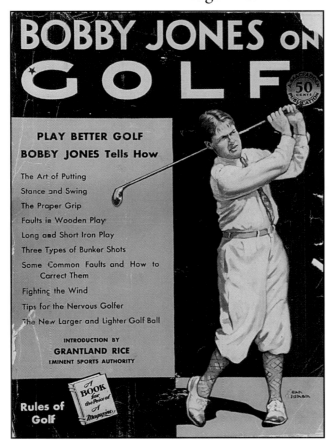

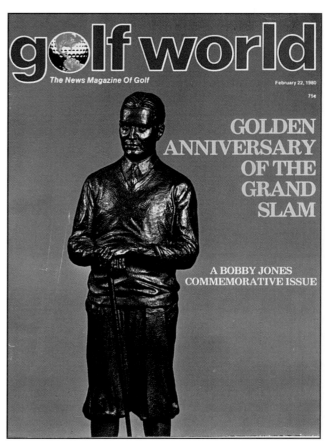

Commemorative Magazine Covers Featuring Bob Jones.

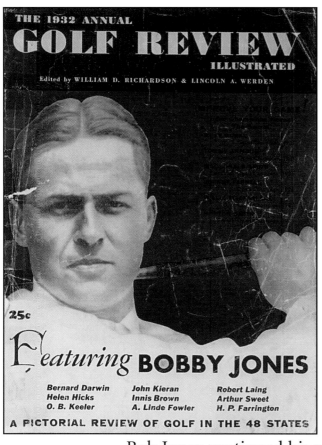

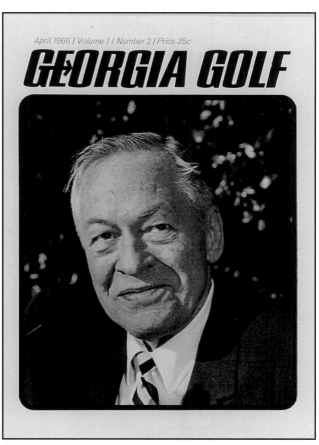

Bob Jones continued his popularity even in later years.

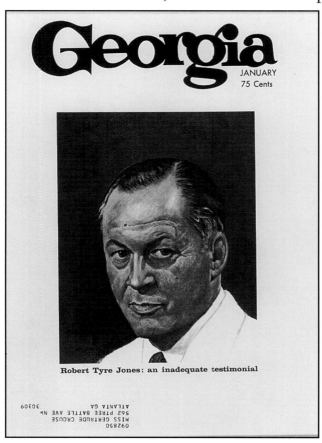

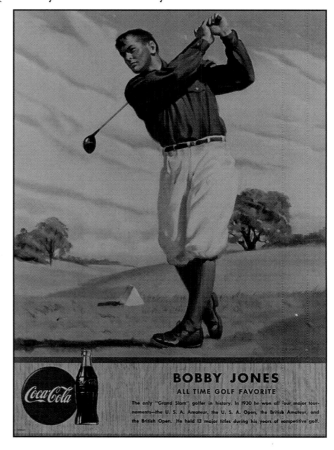

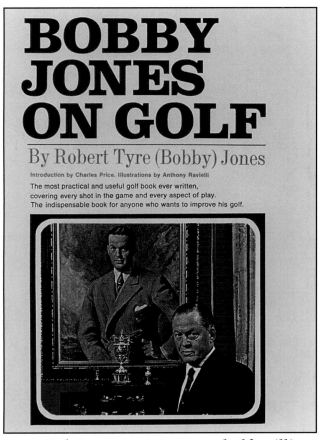

Bob Jones wrote over a half-million words in various books and periodicals.

Chapter 9
Bobby Jones in Hollywood

The world was his stage. The finest and most testing golf links and courses set the scenes. His audiences were populated not only with the golfing faithful, but also the common man who Alistair Cooke notes, *"didn't know the difference between a golf club and a stair rod."* This actor, though not traditionally schooled in Shakespearean techniques, was carefully prepared by the school of experience, if not hard knocks. Surely proper training embraces the feat of a 6-year-old who faithfully mimicked the impeccable technique of Stewart Maiden's Carnoustie swing. There was no need for this actor to pretend or imagine what it would be like to accomplish heroics in the face of impossible circumstances. This actor already had compiled the "credits" from a wealth of experience before he even took the stage. So it was not surprising that when he conquered Hollywood, the stars themselves were among the first to cast their crowns. Unlike the others, his stage name and real name were the same: Bobby Jones.

In a city nicknamed "Tinsel Town," it is difficult to distinguish phony from real, hyperbole from literal, sincerity from pretense. Bob Jones brought to Hollywood the genuine article. Rarely before had Hollywood seen a truly shy and humble man, who, Atlanta's Ralph McGill observed, *"never took himself or his feats seriously enough to stuff his shirt with them."* It was not without some tradeoffs, however, that Bob resolved to come to Hollywood in the first place.

Prior to 1930, having built a reputation in his sport such that the oddsmakers would often put the entire field against him, Jones knew he would one day retire from competition. He also would eschew a professional golf career while stating his rationale:

I suppose I have often been called a jackass because I have not seen fit to play professional golf. I am commended in some quarters for mastering the ideals of amateur sport and censured in others for foolishly refusing to grasp the bonanza of wealth supposed to be waiting for me if I should turn pro. Yet although I began to play golf quite by accident and played for years without exactly knowing why, I have had very definite reasons for not accepting golf as a profession; but the idealistic part of the thing is entirely apart from that decision.

Why then did Jones quit?

Bob appreciated the professional calling since he himself had been practicing law professionally since 1928, when he passed the bar exam in his first year at Emory Law School. As he said:

If enough people will pay money to see Walter Hagen play golf to make it profitable for him to play, and if he wants to play, I cannot see why the situation is vastly different from that of Caruso's being paid to sing or of a lawyer's drafting a contract...The calling is a legitimate one and there appears to be no good reason why a man should not accept it if he desires.

Rather than sacrifice what he viewed as the pleasures of golf in order to make it his business, Bob chose instead to follow the law. The "grind" of playing for pay did not appeal to him either:

I had found out the vast difference between playing golf for pleasure and golf as a business, and that professional golf involved considerably more than long putts and twenty-dollar bills. I had learned that a good many pros who had full-time positions with clubs, where they maintained a shop and gave lessons, earned comfortable livings, but that the only men who drew really attractive incomes were those in demand for exhibition purposes. And I also had learned something of what exhibition tours meant and I did not like them.

Night after night on Pullmans, and round after round of golf played before thundering crowds, with no chance for relaxation and little possibility of enjoying what the rest of us think of as home. And when the tournament season arrives it means more traveling at one's own expense in an effort to win more titles in order to induce more invitations to exhibition games.

It should be explained that the rules permitted amateur golfers to retain their status when paid for writing in publications. Jones had been paid by the Bell Syndicate to write a weekly golf column in the late 1920s under the byline, "My Theory of Golf" and "Bobby Jones Says." The rule legalized such activity on the grounds that writing was not teaching or playing the game for a consideration, and its value was focused on the knowledge of the writer rather than the actual playing of it.

Until the "Great Year of 1930," when Hollywood came calling with staggering offers for doing films, Bob had no trouble saying *No*. He had plenty of practice turning down myriad offers whose principal purpose was not the advancement of golfing mankind, but rather the blatant increase of the gross national product and financial status of the promoters. If any lasting significance was possessed by such deals, it was sorely lost on Bob. So Bob wrote his books and articles and remained an amateur. The economic opportunity cost was not insignificant. Grantland Rice estimated that Jones' victories cost the professionals almost $30,000 annually in lost winnings.

After the Grand Slam was in the history books, Bob made this statement to explain why he no longer felt enjoined from what was clearly a commercial endeavor:

Upon the close of the 1930 golfing season I determined immediately that I would withdraw entirely from golfing competition of a serious nature. Fourteen years of intense tournament play in this country and abroad had given me about all I wanted in the way of hard work in the game. I had reached a point where I felt that my profession required more of my time and effort, leaving golf in its proper place, a means of obtaining recreation and enjoyment.

My intention at the time was to make no announcement of retirement, but merely to drop out quietly by neglecting to send in my entry to the open championship next spring. There was at that time no reason to make a definite statement of any kind, but since then, after careful consideration, I have decided upon a step which I think ought to be explained to the golfers of this country, in order that they may have a clear understanding of what the thing is and why it is being done.

On November 13, 1930, I signed a contract with Warner Brothers Pictures to make a series of twelve one-reel motion pictures, devoted entirely to exhibiting and explaining the methods which I employ in playing the shots ordinarily required in playing a round of golf. These pictures are to be purely educational in character, and it is the ardent hope of both parties that they will be of some value, first by improving the play and thereby increasing the enjoyment of the vast number of people already interested in the game, and, second, by creating an interest where none exists now among the many who may find enjoyment and beneficial exercise on the golf course.

The talking picture, with its combination of visual presentation and demonstration, with the possibility of detailed explanation, appeals to me as the ideal vehicle for an undertaking of this nature.

Of course, the matter of monetary compensation enters into the discussion at this point, and it is for numerous reasons that I wish to be perfectly understood on this score. The amateur status problem is one of the most serious with which the United States Golf Association has to deal for the good of the game as a whole.

I am not certain that the step I am taking is in a strict sense a violation of the amateur rule. I think a lot might be said on either side. But I am so far convinced that it is contrary to the spirit of amateurism that I am prepared to accept and even endorse a ruling that it is an infringement.

I have chosen to play as an amateur not because I have regarded an honest professionalism as discreditable, but because I have had other ambitions in life. So long as I played as an amateur there could be no question of subterfuge or concealment. The rules of the game, whatever they were, I have respected, sometimes even beyond the letter. I certainly shall never become a professional golfer. But, since I am no longer a competitor, I feel able to act entirely outside the amateur rule, as my judgment and conscience may decide.

When these pictures have been made, I expect to return to the practice of my profession, unhampered by the necessity of keeping my golf up to championship requirements.

Jones limited his major commercial activities to these films, a golf radio show sponsored by Listerine, and a lengthy contractual deal with Spalding as a golf-club designer. Bob never changed his puritan proclivity to steer away from golf commercialism. He would never be remembered in the same paragraph with the "million dollar" golfers of today, whose place in history is marked by total income rather than singular accomplishment.

On November 13, 1930, Jones signed a contract with Warner Brothers for considerably less than the quarter-million dollars reported in the newspapers. When previously asked by a reporter at Merion, *"Have you signed a movie contract for a quarter of a million dollars?"* Jones replied, *"Get me such a contract and I shall certainly sign it."* He did sign, but the final version paid Bob only $120,000 for "How I Play Golf." The money was placed in a trust fund for Bob's children. In the end, however, royalties and a second series of six reels would indeed reach the quarter-million mark.

Warner Brothers shrewdly tapped a single-digit handicap golfer for the director position in the person of George E. Marshall. Marshall had considerable experience producing serial shows with the notion of moviegoers coming back each week to see the sequential and suspenseful story lines.

The stars in these serials included Tom Mix, Ruth Roland, Harry Carey, and William Russell; and the series included The Perils of Pauline and Mack Sennett comedies. Marshall played competent golf at Lakeside Golf Club, which would give him a necessary technical perspective in directing the films.

Lakeside was where Bob was first indoctrinated by Douglas Fairbanks on his inaugural visit to Hollywood. That first match, not unlike similar experiences, began simply enough as a private outing with only caddies to report the outcome. Within the first several holes, when word had leaked out, hundreds of local spectators arrived in their cars and thus converted private recreation into spectacle. Jones should have suspected as much from his friend Fairbanks.

Fairbanks was an ardent Jones fan and spent many important occasions with him. He had invented a peculiar game popularized with his name "Doug," which Jones adopted as his physical training to lose weight in preparation for the Date with Destiny in 1930. The game was played with badminton-like racquets over a tennis-style net and court (set up at the Atlanta theater) with both players trying to keep a shuttlecock in the air long enough to approximate, if not achieve, aerobic exhaustion. It certainly achieved its purpose, for Bob was in fine physical fettle at the start of the 1930 campaign. In later years Jones even built an indoor court in the backyard of his Tuxedo Road estate in Atlanta.

It was also Fairbanks and his Hollywood cronies who gave Bob a psychological boost on the voyage to Britain that year. Fairbanks looked into the camera and wished Bob the *"best of luck in Great Britain this spring"* in a reel to be seen in all the movie houses. Vaudeville star Harry Lauder, dressed in a kilt, was then asked if he planned to play golf too. *"No,"* Lauder explained, *"I am going to go fishing."* When Fairbanks inquired further if he still played golf, Lauder, winking at Jones out of the corner of his eye, replied in thick Scottish brogue, *"No, I lost ma' baal tew' years ago."* Jones loved the repartee. Famous stars including Richard (Dick) Arlen, Harold Lloyd, and Earnest and David Torrance played at Lakeside.

Marshall astutely arranged three cameras to whir at varying angles to capture the most information possible from the Jones films. In one series, a camera angle was established directly in front of the ascending trajectory of longer clubs so that the ball was seen whizzing overhead while the viewer "ducked" the shot in the theater. One of Bob's shots, however, actually hit the camera dead on and put out its eye, prompting the announcer to exclaim that such deadly accuracy required replacement of *"yet another camera!"*

To assist in creating the storylines, O.B. Keeler was brought on board the film crew as an "advisor." Keeler was himself as extraordinary a character as any that Hollywood had ever seen. Called "Pop" by his friends and fellow reporters, Keeler was a respected newspaper man by the time he saw Jones win his first Georgia state tournament at age 14.

Keeler could tell a story better than anybody, and because of his "tarbucket" mind (everything that went in stuck), he was able to recite both classical and ribald prose and poetry at the drop of a hat. Even Bernard Darwin found Keeler irrepressible. When these two titans of world literature found themselves in a quoting match on a boat voyage from Southampton to New London, it was Darwin who readily conceded defeat while shaking his head in disbelief.

Keeler traveled 120,000 miles with Jones, including three times each to Europe and California. During one stretch, Keeler wrote more than 500 golf columns for the *Associated Press* and was dubbed Bobby Jones "Boswell" for having chronicled 31 tournaments. Keeler personally witnessed all thirteen of the major titles won by Jones, a feat that Bob's own father, Colonel Bob, did not match. Keeler often liked to remark that "despite the poor newspaper pay," he still enjoyed it so much that he felt he was taking money "under false pretenses." Keeler was the first reporter to be granted an interview by the Prince of Wales on golf and was also the first ever to broadcast a sporting event across the Atlantic Ocean — the British Open Golf Championship of 1930.

Keeler frequently appeared on NBC Radio in Atlanta. He once engineered a hilarious broadcast interview with the Metropolitan Opera's famous tenor, Giovanni Martinelli. At that time Atlanta was a "dry" town, so Martinelli brought enough booze from New York to fill up his hotel bathtub. Keeler was known to bend an elbow or two in his day, and he and the singer got quite a snoot full before they went on the air. By the time the show ended, Keeler had corrupted the tenor into performing a duet with him on the air. And the party didn't stop when the show ended. Keeler squired Martinelli to the better night spots of Atlanta, and they returned only when the sidewalks were rolled up in the wee hours of the morning.

Pop was not averse to drinking and gambling. He nicknamed his home on North Avenue in Atlanta "Distillery Hill." He was fired from his last job before becoming a reporter for negotiating a $5 bet on a baseball game after his boss prohibited gambling. In addition to his love of serious literature, Pop exercised his inventive mind by making up risque limericks and poems. He was once asked to introduce a nationally prominent speaker at a University of Georgia function. When the speaker sent word that he was delayed by the weather, Pop began to kill time by making up limericks. The more he told, the dirtier the limericks got. By the time the speaker arrived, the audience was on its feet, raucously clapping and shouting for Keeler to keep going. After seeing all this, the speaker didn't even want to go on.

Jones, the shy, classy gentleman and genius golfer, was an astonishing contrast to his roommate Keeler, the gregarious hard-drinking newspaper man. However, both enjoyed a good laugh and practical joke. During one exhibition match between Walter Hagen and Jones, Hagen's ball found its way into a bunker.

Bob furtively handed his caddie one of the old giant federal $20 bills and told him to crumple it up and toss it into the bunker next to Hagen's ball. When Hagen prepared for his trap shot, he saw the bill and, of course, picked it up and put it in his pocket as fluidly as if it were part of his pre-shot routine. He was disqualified on that hole, however, because of the rule forbidding the removal of any loose impediments in a hazard. The humorous mischief of the episode was not lost on the players or the spectators.

After one of Jones' victories, he and his entourage enjoyed the hospitality of an admiring friend who entertained them in his palatial estate. Pop made his usual contributions to the life of the party and suffered for it the next morning with something akin to *"cocktail flu."* Pop explained that he *"felt like hell hit with a ripe tomato."* The hostess of the estate recognized Pop's malady, and she sent a butler up to his room with a bracer dubbed a *"whisky punch"* comprised of milk generously laced with bourbon whisky. After quaffing the mixture, Keeler flashed his trademark grin at Jones and commented on his instant revitalization: *"This is the finest milk I ever drank, Bobby. If I could find the cow that gave it, I would marry her myself."*

Jones told that story more than once on Keeler. Pop's spontaneity was almost limitless. Once Pop spied the iceman lugging a 100-pound block of ice with a pair of tongs into Crawford's Beanery Restaurant in Atlanta. As if he were the iceman's superior, Pop insisted, *"I want to borrow that ice to conduct a scientific experiment."* Keeler then put the ice on an adjacent weighing machine which, in return for inserting a penny, ejected a card which gave the weight on the scales and something about the nature of the person being weighed. Pop gleefully put the penny in and pulled out the card. Of course a small crowd gathered around as Pop read the card: *"You are a warm and kindly nature. You love to sing and dance. WEIGHT: 80 pounds."* The small crowd got a big laugh, except for perhaps the iceman who was caught in the act of shorting the restaurant owner by 20 pounds of ice. With Pop and Jones on board in Hollywood, Marshall had his hands full.

When the questions got tough, Bob could rely on O.B. to take the heat for him. For instance, when pushed to answer whether he was going to quit golf before the Grand Slam was even in the books, Bob turned to O.B. *"You know. Tell them."* O.B. then tapped into his vast literary reservoir and recited:

If I ever become a rich man,

or if ever I grow to be old

I will build a house with deep thatch

to shelter me from the cold,

I will hold my house in the high woods

within a walk of the sea,

And the men that were boys

when I was a boy

shall sit and drink with me.

There were no follow-up questions.

Marshall sought to make the instructional films in an informal, conversational vein which both Jones and he felt would be better accepted by amateur audiences. Bob reflected his instinctual gift for sensitivity concerning the theme of the films and insisted that they be titled, "How I Play Golf." He thought it presumptuous to assert that there was only one way to play the game and genuinely wished only to add his philosophy and techniques for what each player assessed their worth.

I do not mean to insist that these methods are the only ones or even that they are the best. But I do think there are certain fundamentals which are the same for all golfers, and in making my explanations I have tried to separate these fundamentals from mannerisms that might be peculiar to my own individual style. The average golfer is not interested in winning championships. The chief benefits of the game for him must be recreation and the companionship of congenial friends. But I've always thought that if the game was worth playing at all it was worth making some effort to play correctly.

Marshall summed it up: *"Most of all we want to make each picture appear natural and spontaneous as though it was something which might have happened during any afternoon's golf game or during a conversation at the club house."* Indeed these films made a timeless record of the magic revealed in Jones' technique which defied written description and caused the viewer to marvel that he had seen what was thought to be impossible.

Perhaps the best word image of Jones' swing was crafted by Bernard Darwin:

I first saw the swing soon to be familiar in the imagination of the whole golfing world; so swift, in that it occupied so little time with no suspicion of waggle, and yet so leisurely in its almost drowsy grace, so lithe and so smooth.

* * *

Of how he actually struck the ball, I think the photographs must convey even to those who never saw him something at least of the matchless beauty and rhythm.

* * *

There could be no more fascinating player to watch not only for the free and rhythmic character of his swing but for the swiftness with which he played. He had as brief a preliminary address as Duncan himself, but there was nothing hurried or slapdash about it and the swing itself if not positively slow, had a certain drowsy beauty which gave the feeling of slowness.

Bob left for California on February 24 and was accompanied by O.B. Keeler, Mrs. Keeler, and Thomas B. Paine, who was past president of the Atlanta Athletic Club and executive committee member in the USGA.

At the train station in Atlanta, all the baggage had been assembled on the platform. Included with the usual trunks and suitcases were 11 separate typewriter boxes. This unusual detail was not lost on Keeler's son, George, who was present to see "Pop" Keeler off to Hollywood, the city of celebrities. In the midst of the excitement of this bon voyage, George casually and quite innocently queried O.B. *"Pop, I know that you plan to work mighty hard in California on these movies but do you really feel that it is going to require 11 typewriters to do the job?"* The elder Keeler quickly and curtly responded as if to preserve a reporter's confidence, *"Quiet George, these are all full of corn liquor!"* Enough said about the preparations for the trip.

If the happy hours had been pre-arranged, it is noteworthy that the script had not. However, during the pre-production meeting at East Lake, Bob did outline to Marshall a general overview of what should be accomplished.

Bob's idea was to start the discussion with the putter, Calamity Jane, and work up the progression of clubs to the driver. Jones would focus on golf theory and mechanics. Keeler, whose inventive mind served as the catalyst for myriad golfing columns, would sit right on the set and hand type the humorous story lines that served as the entree for Jones instruction.

Not only did Warner Brothers celebrities jump at the chance to become beneficiaries of Bob's golf lessons, but the celebrities of other studios sought and were granted special releases to participate in these endeavors. The astonishing fact was that none were paid except Jones. The various studios acted from a considered motive that the numerous celebrities would increase their currency among the national audiences simply by their association with Bob in these reels. They were not mistaken in such assessments.

Richard Arlen, fighter pilot star in a then-popular film, Wings, confirmed,

Paramount allowed me to go over and do this short because of the esteem they had for Bobby Jones. It was a loan that wasn't often done in those days. It was probably the greatest two weeks I ever spent.

Marshall remembered it in the same way: *"We had a wonderful time. The top actors and actresses donated their time. All of the stars were eager to take part. It was a privilege to have Jones work on their game."*

Jones agreed. *"Did I enjoy it? Hell yes. I'll never forget it. There was a story line in each episode, but we didn't have a script — they made it up as we went along. The plots wound up at the end of each 10-minute short, and there was a lot of horseplay and comedy, with the instructional business woven in."*

The storylines pounded out by Keeler were simple, witty, and fun. Jones' putting lesson is set up when Joe E. Brown refuses to concede a short putt which is missed by Frank Craven:

FRANK — *Now, wait a minute. Going to give me this, are you?*

JOE — *Give it to you?*

FRANK — *Sure. This little one.*

JOE — *You mean, concede it.*

FRANK — *Yeah.*

JOE — *I made mine, didn't I? Shoot.*

FRANK — *All right; all right; if that's the way you feel about it.*

JOE — *Nice putt, Frank. Don't forget the balls.*

DICK — *Oh, Frank. Come here a minute. I want you to know Bobby Jones.*

FRANK — *Oh, how do you do, Mr. Jones.*

BOBBY — *Glad to meet you, Mr. Craven.*

FRANK — *I'm glad to know you, sir. Did you see what happened over there?*

BOBBY — *I certainly did; it was hard luck.*

FRANK — *'Um — just that long. The big buzzard wouldn't give it to me.*

BOBBY — *Well, you know the object of the game is to get the ball into the hole. These little short putts count just as much as a longer one.*

FRANK — *Do you miss many like that?*

BOBBY — *Well, a good many, but I practice hard on them.*

FRANK — *The little ones, too?*

FRANK — *Want to do me a favor?*

BOBBY — *I'd like to.*

FRANK — *Come on over here. Show me how you do those things, will you?*

At some point in each of the reels, the actors turned to "Doctor" Bobby Jones to help diagnose their golfing afflictions and to prescribe the appropriate and preferably instant cure. Charles Winninger beats his usual foursome to the golf course by an hour and a half so he can get help on his chip shots. When his playing partners show up, they learn a little something too. The episode on the niblick is prompted after a wealthy industrialist comes home late complaining to his wife about his day-long problems "at the office." After eliciting feigned sympathy, his wife reveals that she already knew the source of his fatigue was a lesson on the use of the niblick administered by Bob Jones. With the fib out in the open, the wife then chastises her husband for refusing to listen to Jones:

VIVIAN — *Terrible day at the office. I suppose you were excavating until darkness overtook you.*

HUNTLEY — *Oh, be reasonable, dear. Bob was showing me that shot with the niblick that I've had so much trouble with; but when he got through with me I made some of the best shots I've ever made in my life.*

VIVIAN — *Why, from where I was sitting on the porch I could see that you didn't do one thing that Bobby told you to.*

HUNTLEY — *Well, what did I do wrong?*

VIVIAN — *Wait a minute. You — you took a short stab at it – u'mm – like that. And you know Bobby always tells you take the club back far enough for the shot. Now, look....!*

(Butler enters, just in time to catch full force of swing on the filled tray!)

In other reels, Jones rescues Leon Errol, who continues to hit the wrong club into the same tree and the ball rebounds backwards. Bob shows Errol that the proper club is the mashie niblick and the ball easily sails over the tree. "The Big Irons" businessman Guy Kibbee sneaks away from the office to *"get some fresh air"* and ends up on the golf course. He is hit by an errant shot, struck by one of his own employees who has also sneaked out for the day. It is only the diplomatic golfing lesson by Jones that quells the boss' anger and saves the employee's job. In a similar way, Bob's focus on "the spoon, brassie, and driver" keeps Zelma O'Neal from divorcing her husband because he has neglected her for his golf. Even the kids are the beneficiary of Jones' techniques. Five-year-old Georgie is abandoned by the older boys, and Jones takes him out on the practice range to cheer him up. The other kids catch up later and vigorously question Jones about his game. Meanwhile, Georgie falls asleep and, at the end of the lesson, is carried in Jones' arms back to the clubhouse.

In the same way that Walter Hagen showed how difficult it was to hit an easy shot, Jones showed how easy it was to hit a difficult shot. The audience didn't have to be an expert in golf theory to understand Jones' advice:

I think the average golfer would be far better off if he would forget all about overswinging. Now, watch the length of my swing with the driver. The trouble with most of them is that they don't take the club back far enough.

* * *

I never go on a practice tee unless I have a definite purpose in view--some correction to make--and I continue only so long as I can keep my mind on what I am doing.

* * *

With the medium irons and short irons, the trouble that I have most often is failing to cock my wrists at the top. I am inclined sometimes to hang on to the club a little bit too tightly so that I don't get that nice rhythm.

The thing to be careful of in the wind is to see that you don't let it rattle you. It baits you into pressing. When you're driving against a stiff breeze, you should take things a bit more easily than usual. Don't try to overcome the wind, but just accept your loss of distance and hit the ball comfortably down the fairway.

* * *

A golfer doesn't need to fix himself on the ground so he is immovable, because the only thing that can upset him is his own swing.

* * *

Now, when it comes to hitting the ball — and this applies to any kind of shot--remember that form is efficiency. The important thing is to select a club with which the distance can be covered comfortably without pressing.

* * *

I always try to emphasize the importance of an ample back-swing. We see so many golfers who begin hitting before they reach the top of the swing. They go back fast and then they get in such a rush to hit the ball that they yank the club down before they fairly get it back. I never play well unless I swing back slowly and make certain of reaching the top before I start down.

* * *

I don't try to putt with my body, but I never try to keep my body still. I'd like it to be free so it can move if the stroke demands it. The whole idea it seems to me is to do the thing in the simplest and most natural way.

Director George Marshall used numerous innovative filming techniques in demonstrating Jones' theories. As an example, Jones was photographed while wearing clothes which were half black on one side of his body and half white on the other side. With the camera facing in front of Jones' swing, the viewer was better able to see the movement of the left half of Jones' body clothed in white. He was also filmed in an all-white costume against a black background. The contrast between Jones' two-tone clothing and the varying backgrounds helped the viewer understand the mechanics of the swing.

The film series was immensely popular at the box office. Even though the moviegoers did not see every episode, there was enough continuity to be enjoyable. Twenty to 30 million viewers in 6,000 movie houses witnessed the first 12 reels. Thereafter, Warner Brothers signed Jones to another six reels produced in 1933 entitled, "How to Break 90." Interestingly, the films did well at the movies even when the bottom dropped out of the movie short business during the depression. The viewers had the same reaction to Jones' swing as W.C. Fields, who shook his head and droned in his classic nasal tone, *"I still don't believe it."*

While the films were popular at the box office, they did not sell well to private individuals. The entire set of 18 reels was expensive and bulky. Serious golfers were distracted by the comic relief scenes. As late as 1968, a Sports Illustrated article entitled, "The Reel Life of Bobby Jones," reported that only one complete set of the films was known to exist. The version deposited with the Library of Congress for copyright entitlement apparently disappeared. Warner Brothers had retained a set, but it would not be rediscovered until 20 years later. None of the movie libraries or museums in Hollywood kept a set either. However, Atlanta banker Mills Lane gave his original set to Jones, and he provided them to his Peachtree Golf Club in Atlanta. Only in recent years, Sybervision has reintroduced these films, which are commercially available and still enjoyable today.

Jones did not spend all his time in Hollywood in front of a movie camera. As a new member of the acting ranks, Bob was adopted by Hollywood's golfing society dubbed the "Divot Diggers" and whose membership was comprised of Hollywood's producers, directors, writers, and technical people. Bob and Mary Jones were special guests of the president and general manager of the Fine Arts Studio, Nat Deverich and his wife. Deverich was also president of the Motion Picture Golfing Association which originated at the San Gabriel Country Club. During one casual Saturday afternoon outing with the Divot Diggers, Bob started to tee up a ball at the first hole. He turned to Roy Phillips, tossed him the new ball he had just taken out of the box, and said, *"That ball isn't round."* Bob then opened a brand new box, picked out another ball, and again said, *"That ball isn't round either. I'll drive it."* Jones teed up the ball and hit a huge drive, but the ball made a curve to the right and then sharply to the left. With a slight grin, Bob then picked yet a third ball, pronounced it round, and hit a terrific drive carrying a water hazard 240 yards from the tee.

The Divot Diggers had a usual game Sunday afternoon at the Flintridge Country Club course. Jones played one afternoon with professional Leo Diegel, pro at Agua Caliente Golf Club, and amateurs Jim Oviatt and Nat Deverich. Unbeknownst to Jones, Diegel and Deverich had arranged for a professional comic named Vince Barnett to caddie for Jones' partner, Oviatt. It was a game unlike any that Jones had known. On the first hole, Jones congenially suggested that his partner needed a No. 2 iron to reach the first green. Bob was jolted when Oviatt's caddie expressed open resentment at Bob's advice and insisted that his player use a No. 5 iron even though the caddie didn't know the difference between a putter and a driver. Of course, Oviatt followed Jones' advice over that of his caddie, but the shot was strong and went over the green. The caddie reacted by openly laughing at Jones' mistaken judgment of distance. The other players, who were in on the practical joke, tried to ignore the needle being given to Jones. On the greens, the caddie "inadvertently" allowed his shadow to cast over the putting line of Jones and made sure that he audibly scoffed if Jones' tee shots were even slightly off line. After Jones slightly hooked one drive, the caddie advised openly, *"Quit pressing."* When none of his playing partners reacted, Jones took the high road of diplomacy and said nothing.

Bob had an especially difficult downhill approach shot on the 5th hole and carefully took his stance. The quiet drama of the backswing was then interrupted by the caddie who had "tripped" causing a cacophony of clanging clubs to spill all over the fairway. Everyone else laughed, but Jones simply glared at the caddie. *"What do you want to use a brassie for; use a spoon,"* the caddie belted out on the sixth.

On the 13th tee, the caddie casually removed a club from Leo Diegel's bag and began to take practice swings with it. With a violent swing, the clubhead crashed into the turf and Diegel's club broke into three pieces. Bob was unaware that before the round started, Diegel "planted" the trick club in his bag. Consolingly, Jones looked at Diegel and said, *"I hope it wasn't a good club."* Then Bob turned to his own caddie and said, *"Don't let that fellow handle any of my clubs."* Thereafter, Diegel cosmetically rebuked his caddie, extracted an apology, and the practical joke continued. Toward the end of the match, Jones was strolling toward his tee shot while having a private congenial chat with Oviatt. The obstreperous caddie rudely butted in to ask of Jones why he quit tournament golf and retired. Before getting an answer the caddie gave the needle again, *"Maybe you'se afraid now that Sarazen is coming so fast, eh?"*

Even with all the distractions, Jones and his partner were in position to win the match at the final par-5 green. Bob crashed two prodigious wood shots leaving himself a critical wee pitch to the flag for the win. There was a pregnant pause while Jones snapped on his trademark concentration for the shot, but he was interrupted by the caddie again:

"Please, Mr. Jones," he muttered in his choicest dialect, *"please ordergraph dis score card."*

"Don't interrupt me now," pleaded Jones. But that caddie was persistent.

"Please ordergraph it now before you make dis big shot," he insisted.

"Well, give me a pencil," moaned Jones as he surrendered.

It was then that O.B. Keeler provided the requested pencil and let Jones in on the joke. Bob was especially good natured about the trick when he was told that "Caddie" Barnett once "ribbed" Pres. Calvin Coolidge in a staged argument over whether better shoes are made in Brockton, Massachusetts, or in Czechoslovakia.

As he had done since the 1917 Red Cross matches, Bob generously contributed his talents for charity events during his stay in California. William Wrigley, Jr., sponsored one tournament on Catalina Island dubbed the Bobby Jones Amateur Golf Tournament. Bob presented the inaugural trophy to the winner. On Sunday, March 12, 1933, Jones and Leo Diegel teamed up against McDonald Smith and George Von Elm for an exhibition at the Wilshire Country Club in Los Angeles. Substantial publicity was created because all proceeds were to be given to popular local professional Chick Fraser, who had cancer, and noted golf writer Eddie Lawrence, who was hospitalized with tuberculosis.

As excitement mounted for the coming match, three consecutive "disasters" struck. First, five days before the match, President Roosevelt declared a bank holiday and every bank in America was closed. Sponsors were fearful that none of the gallery could afford the dollar entry fee. Then, two days before the match, the worst earthquake in Los Angeles history hit, killing and injuring hundreds of people. Having never suffered through an earthquake, Jones became violently nauseated and even the aftershocks affected him such that he was unable to eat. Von Elm had his own problems; he suffered with pleurisy, but insisted on going through with the match despite sharp chest pains and having one whole side taped up.

As if the circumstances weren't complicated enough, a tremendous rain storm completely waterlogged the Wilshire's fairways, and the barranca which meandered through the course became a knee-deep river. To the surprise of the promoters, almost 3,000 spectators showed up to see the action anyway. Even natural disasters would not stop them from seeing the great Jones. They hawked his every move, even though Mac Smith and Von Elm had the match won at the 17th by a 2 to 1 margin.

Not pleased with his performance, Bob very much wanted to win the final hole. With his partner, Diegel, out of the hole, and both his opponents safely on the green, Bob went for the knockout shot which skipped over the green instead. Several thousand spectators, including golfwriter for the *L.A. Herald Express*, Darsie L. Darsie, crowded around to see Bob's ball submerged in four inches of water in a barranca behind the green. A.P. executive Brian Bell, an ardent Jones follower, whispered, *"He'll play it."* The crowd was delighted at Jones' resolve to conquer this difficulty. They craned their necks as Jones slid one foot knee deep into the water and propped his other foot on the muddy bank. His furrowed brow relaxed a moment as he permitted a half smile to crease his lips. Everyone could sense the excitement and tension generated from the task at hand. This is what everyone came for. This is what golf is all about. With trademark rhythm and seemingly slow motion, Bob's niblick glided back and crashed down causing an explosion of mud and water into the air ejecting the ball to within four feet of the hole. The electrified roar of the crowd showed their absolute delight for the privilege of witnessing Jones' proper diagnosis of the difficulty and perfection in administering the remedy. Bob permitted a modest grin as he wiped enough splattered mud from his face to see what had happened to the ball. These witnesses would surely testify repeatedly to others that only the great Bobby Jones could have pulled it off. And they were there to see it — the shot of a lifetime. Never mind that he missed the putt! The play's the thing. And Jones knew how to play.

Chapter 10
Matinee Idol,
"Bobby Jones"

SPALDING'S
ATHLETIC LIBRARY

GOLF Guide
1931

Robert
Tyre
Jones
Jr.

Edited by
GRANTLAND
RICE

UNITED
STATES
AMATEUR
CHAMPION

1924 1925
1927 1928 1930

UNITED STATES
OPEN
CHAMPION

1923 1926
1929 1930

BRITISH OPEN
CHAMPION

1926 1927

BRITISH
AMATEUR
CHAMPION

American Sports
Publishing
Company 45 Rose St.
New York

Bobby Jones announced his retirement from competitive golf on November 17, 1930 in a carefully prepared statement:

Fourteen years of intense tournament play in this country and abroad have given me about all I wanted in the way of hard work in the game. I had reached the point where I felt that my profession required more of my time and effort, leaving golf in its proper place, a means of obtaining recreation and enjoyment.

Upon learning of Jones' announcement, King Edward VIII of England said, *"He has done more than any other golfer ever has done before, and more, I am convinced, than any other golfer will do again."*

Jones announced that he was engaging in several business ventures which could be construed as a violation of the amateur status rule. *"I am so far convinced that it is contrary to the spirit of amateurism that I am prepared to accept and even endorse a ruling that it is an infringement,"* Jones said. *The British Daily Mail* hailed the American as the *"complete embodiment of the grand old golfing spirit, the decline of which is often deplored. He is so staunch a conservative that he has scarcely even tried steel shafts. Hickory is good enough for him."* The *British News Chronicle* added, *"Jones' personal charm and his modesty in triumph are assets which make him an invaluable traveling advertisement of the finer and rarer qualities of the American race."* He also resigned from the executive committee of the USGA, an office which he had held since 1928, and for which he had been renominated. Bob's first venture was to deliver 26 weekly broadcasts on golf over WSB/NBC Radio, sponsored by the Lambert Pharmaceutical Company, makers of Listerine.

Radio announcer Bill Munday spoke standing in the introduction and conclusion, and during Bobby's talk, he slipped out into the control room. Bobby heard the door open and close toward the end of his own talk and didn't know what it was. When Bill explained later, Bobby said, *"For goodness sake don't do that again. I thought somebody was coming in to choke me off!"* Bobby prepared his own talks following the same chronological order adhered to in his book, *"Down the Fairway."* *"I think we'll all have a lot of fun out of it,"* Bob said of his work.

You know, golf is a funny game. There never was a round of golf played in a big championship or just among friends, by experts or duffers, that didn't develop its humorous situations, and often really dramatic interludes. I've enjoyed golf a lot, and I'm enjoying it more in retrospect. The game looks a great deal more attractive to me since I am out of the competitive end of it. That was always grueling work, and it bore down pretty savagely toward the end.

On November 13, 1930, Bob Jones signed a contract with Warner Brothers Pictures to make a series of 12 one-reel motion pictures devoted entirely to exhibiting and explaining the methods employed by Jones in playing a round of golf. Jones explained:

These pictures are to be purely educational in character, and is the ardent hope of both parties that they will be of some value, first by improving the play and thereby increasing the enjoyment of the vast number of people already interested in the game, and second, by creating an interest where none exists now among the many who may find enjoyment and beneficial exercise on the golf course.

217

"Movie star" Bob Jones and the Warner Brothers. (From right) Albert, Jack, and Harry Warner, and Harry's son, Louis. For the first 12 reels, Jones was paid $120,000 plus a percentage of the gross. Half of the proceeds were paid to a trust fund set up for Bob's children and administered by his father, Col. R.P. Jones. Unfortunately, the IRS and Bob did not see eye-to-eye on this arrangement. When the IRS assessed Bob's taxes on the full amount of the proceeds, Bob politely objected because he had only personally received half. When the IRS didn't budge, Bob paid the entire tax bill under protest and sued the government in federal court for a refund. It was the only time Jones was ever defeated twice by the same "person." He received an adverse decision by the U.S. District judge which was affirmed by the U.S. Fifth Circuit Court of Appeals.

Bob Jones got spectacular results for the camera when the script called for demonstrating shots from bad lies. *"All you need here is to get your angle right,"* Bob said. *"I use a lofted club and strike under the ball so it will rebound over the face of the club without touching it. If you get close to the hole you're lucky, of course, but there is always a chance."*

Warner Brothers had the foresight to also retain Atlanta's O.B. Keeler to help create the storylines. Starting from scratch, Keeler could bat out a 10-minute storyline on demand and type 10 pages of clean copy an hour. Keeler also helped to narrate some of the stories.

Jones carefully chose the title of the series "How I Play Golf."

It was intended to mean something; for while I have tried to explain the methods which I employ in playing the various shots, I do not mean to insist that these methods are the only ones, or even that they are the best. But I do think that there are certain fundamentals which are the same for all golfers, and in making my explanations I have tried to separate these fundamentals from mannerisms which might be peculiar to my own individual style, in order that what I had to say might be of general application. The average golfer is not interested in winning championships. The chief benefits of the game for him must be recreation and the companionship of congenial friends, but it seems to me that that is little excuse for playing the game in a haphazard way. I have always thought that if a game was worth playing at all, it was worth making some effort to play it correctly.

Chapter 11
Bobby Jones
Greatest Shots…
and Some Others

Even for the greatest golfer who ever played the game, there were the best of shots and there were the worst of shots. For most players, the best shots of their lives might be the holes in one. Bob had two of these. The first was at the No. 11 hole on the No. 1 course at East Lake CC in Atlanta. The second came at the No. 14 hole at the Augusta CC. Neither of these even comes close, however, to the best shots Bob made in his illustrious career, either by his own estimation or critical review. The best shots Bob ever made are steeped in much history. And his worst shots are no less entertaining and noteworthy.

To Bob Jones, a properly executed stroke was merely an *"accident"* and a poorly executed one was *"good exercise."* Such a simplistic philosophy was only distilled from years of internal struggle. However many strokes Bob made in his relatively short 14-year competitive career, the variations in circumstances, expectations, and execution prevented him from hitting two strokes exactly alike.

Those shots which came off perfectly as visualized were met with downcast eyes and a modest smile. As for the others, suffice it to say that some emotions could not be endured with a golf club in his hands. Bernard Darwin, an admiring student of Bob Jones' swing, wrote:

Bobby did hate missing a shot. Perhaps that's why he missed so few, for in the end that highly strung nervous temperament, if it had never been his master, became his invaluable servant. In his most youthful and tempestuous days he had never been angry with his opponent and not often, I think, with Fate, but he had been furiously angry with himself. He set himself an impossibly high standard; he thought it an act of incredible folly if not a positive crime to make a stroke that was not exactly as it ought to be made and as he knew he could make it.

Of course, in championship play, Bob did subdue a *"naturally fiery temper til he played the game outwardly as a man of ice; but the flames still leaped up within."* Later, when Bob would miss a shot in competition, he was simply heard to remark in jest; *"Well, I believe I could have done that well with a lot less preparation."* The best of strokes and the worst of strokes were the product of this emotional evolution.

When Bob's biographer, O.B. Keeler, was asked about Bob's greatest and most important stroke, Keeler described not a mighty blow of 300 yards, but rather a short negotiation of only 4 yards.

The occasion was the final round of the U.S. Open Championship at Winged Foot in 1929. The putt was not for birdie, but rather for par to save Bob from scoring an 80, which he had never done in 10 prior Open championships. The putt was but 12 feet of wickedly curling turf to tie Al Espinosa who had already finished. O.B. Keeler couldn't bear to watch but rejoiced when he heard the thunderous cheer that celebrated the downing of the pressure putt Keeler believed had set Jones on his successful Grand Slam march. Buoyed by the confidence of that putt, Jones defeated Espinosa the following day by 23 strokes in the 36-hole playoff. Eyewitness Al Watrous said the 10-inch breaking putt was so expertly judged that *"if the hole was but a 4¼-inch circle on the green, Bob's ball would have stopped right in the middle."* It was the finest putt Watrous had ever seen; but not the best iron shot Watrous ever saw Bob make.

Instead, the best iron shot both Watrous and Jones ranked tops was made in 1926 in the British Open Championship contested at Royal Lytham and St. Annes. It was such a tight contest between Jones and Watrous that only a stroke separated the pair by the 16th hole of the final round. Jones' drive on the 17th cut the dogleg left and ended in broken sandy ground roughly analogous to a bunker, and positioned him 175 yards from the green where Watrous had safely played his second stroke. Bob sensed the urgency of the moment and selected his No. 4 mashie iron. He then played a stroke that was so delicately executed that Bernard Darwin observed *"a teaspoon too much of sand would have ruined the shot."* The ball finished inside that of Watrous who was so staggered that he three putted and essentially handed the trophy to Bob on that definitive hole. *"There goes a hundred thousand bucks,"* lamented Watrous.

Another bunker shot on the Old Course at St. Andrews played an equally important role in laying the predicate for the most difficult championship victory in Bob's career — the 1930 British Amateur. The format of the Amateur required a player to survive eight matches against eight players, mostly in 18-hole contests at the preliminary stages. At 18 holes, any *"Tom, Dick, or Harry with a hot putter" could put out even the greatest player in the world.* In his first match, Bob drew Sid Roper who hailed from Nottinghamshire and was expected to populate his card more with 5s than any lower numbers. Instead of being a pushover, ex-coal miner Roper posted only a single 5 with his 14 pars and gave Jones the time of his life on the course. By the fifth, hole Jones was 5-under par but only 3 up on the keen Roper. Bob was successful by a 3 and 2 margin, but he freely offered that Roper's superb play could have bested any other contestant in the championship.

The pivotal hole in Bob's judgment, at least the one which steeled his resolve such that he daunted his opponent, was the fourth hole. Bob's drive landed in the enormous Cottage Bunker positioned about 140 yards from the green. Bob holed the shot for an eagle 2! Even though Roper halved the next hole with a birdie 4, Bob made his point and felt that some of the flannel had been extracted from Roper's game effort at an upset. When the match ended on the 16th green, Bob lacked only two 4s on the remaining holes for a 68, which would have equalled the *"wholly indecent"* record he previously set in 1927.

Oddly enough, it was another bunker shot on the 11th hole at St. Andrews which played host to perhaps the worst shot of Jones' illustrious career. *"If made by a lesser man it would have been quickly forgotten,"* said Henry Longhurst. But this was not a lesser man's blunder. The year was 1921, and it was Bob's inaugural pilgrimage to the Old Course. After leading all amateurs after two rounds, except the playoff loser Roger Wethered, Bob played the first nine holes of the third round in a shocking 46. He made 6 at the 10th and drove into Hill bunker with his tee shot on the par-3 11th hole. After several attempts at blasting the ball out, Jones decided the only way the ball was to exit the bunker was in his pocket. Bob tore his scorecard to shreds on the 12th, and, by withdrawing from his only major championship ever, Jones experienced the *"most inglorious failure"* of his golfing life.

Bob played the hole again in 1936 after he sent in a request for a balloted tee time simply with the name *"R.T. Jones, Jr., Atlanta."* When he lunched overlooking the first tee, there were 2,000 spectators lining the fairway. He regretted that his plan to play an informal match had clashed with some scheduled tournament. In fact, the whole town had turned out to see him play, the shopkeepers placing signs in their shops: *"Bobby's Back."* He played a glorious 32 going out and then, at the 11th, bunkered his ball at a spot slightly over the back of the green. In 1958, Jones went back to that place and asked a greenskeeper what happened to the bunker. The greenskeeper replied that there had never been a small bunker over the top of the 11th hole. Jones incredulously responded, *"You can't tell me that because I played two shots from there in 1936!"*

It seems that the bunker shots did present the most difficult challenges to players of the hickory-shaft era. There were at least two methods available to negotiate a bunker with the sharp-edged niblick, which was the implement of choice for the job. Walter Hagen used the skills of a surgeon as he perfected the *"chip"* from the bunker. Jones, and most of the others, used a full or modified *"blast"* shot with the niblick well laid back.

In 1930, Bob was gifted a special club for bunker play by Horton Smith. It had a heavy flange and concave face. The club was known as the concave sand wedge. Bob used the club on only two occasions in 1930. The first shot was simply to extricate his ball from a gorse bush at St. Andrews. The second shot was one of the most remarkable of his lifetime.

During the final round of the Open championship at Hoylake, Bob hit his approach to the 16th hole in the bunker guarding the left side of the green. With his right foot resting on the outside bank of the bunker, Bob was required to loft the ball off the downward slope and elevate it over the formidable bunker face onto a marble-top-fast green. He judged it so perfectly that the ball touched the hole and finished only inches away setting up a birdie 3. No wonder the R&A declared the club illegal immediately thereafter.

That birdie at Hoylake was all the more critical because of a series of blunders which produced a 7 on Bob's card at the par-5 eighth hole. After a fine drive and spoon shot had placed him virtually hole high, Jones took 5 more strokes to get the ball down.

Bernard Darwin later wrote that a *nice old lady with a croquet mallet could have saved him two strokes*. "I took 7 on that hole in the most reasonable manner possible," Bob rationalized. The episode, however unfortunate, had a profound effect on Bob's motivation:

I should like to say that this disaster caused me to rise up in all my might and resolve to win out at all costs. I should like to feel from that point on it was my blazing spirit that carried me to victory.

✳✳✳

I realize that in one brief span of only a moment or two all of the effort of the past three days had just about been washed out. I wasn't looking at any Grand Slam, only at the one championship.

Bob's victory dispelled a commonly held notion that it was not possible to win an Open Championship with a 7 on the card. But, Bob always seemed to have his way with records like that.

In searching for Bob's best strokes, we won't find much from examining his play on par-3 holes. In 10 U.S. Open championships, Bob played 160 par-3 holes but only made a total of 5 birdies. Some observers thought Bob's high draw-type shot was not particularly suited to the one-shotters, especially if the flag was placed tightly on the right edge of the green.

A particularly important example of this difficulty was presented on the 17th hole at the U.S. Open championship played at Interlachen, Minnesota. Bob's brassie tee shot to the 263-yard hole was pushed to the right of the green and caromed off a tree. The USGA official in charge, Prescott Bush, ruled that the ball had gone into a pond. Bob often said that *"the difference between a sand trap and water is the difference between a car crash and an airline crash. You have a chance of recovering from a car crash."* Except Bob could recover from either. Jones was permitted a drop near the green rather than having to play a lost ball from the tee. He made 5 on the hole and came to the 18th green with a single stroke advantage over MacDonald Smith.

A 40-foot putt separated Bob's ball from the hole. He could easily have three-putted the green, but instead the ball went down for a spectacular birdie and a 2-stroke win.

It was not the only time Bob's putting rescued him in the clutch. For instance, Bob sank a 120-foot putt on the fifth hole, a double green, at St. Andrews on his way to his 1927 British Open Championship. And he played perhaps the most perfect round of golf ever in 1926 at Sunningdale. Bob's total was 66 — with 33 putts and 33 other shots.

One of Bob's best putts was in the 1930 match against Cyril Tolley for the British Amateur. Bob had invented a novel approach to the 17th Road Hole by hitting his No. 4 iron to the top of the hole near the 18th tee. His long approach putt was a ghastly 8 feet short. When Tolley's wee pitch was virtually stone dead for a birdie 4, Bob had his back up against the wall. He steeled his nerves and sank the putt. Buoyed by that confidence, Bob defeated Tolley with the aid of a stymie on the first play-off hole.

It did take years for Bob to develop into a superb putter. In his early years as a 14-year-old lad playing his first major championship at Merion CC, Bob actually putted off the sixth green into a creek. He later received a putting lesson from Walter J. Travis, the grand old man of golf, who distinguished himself by defeating the British on their own soil and expatriating the Amateur Trophy to the colonies in 1904 for the first time. When Travis first saw young Jones at Merion playing in his first major championship, Travis remarked that Jones *"would never improve on his shotmaking but might better learn the occasions upon which they should be played...and his putting method was faulty."* A lesson was arranged by Bob's father, the irrepressible Col. Robert P. Jones, but the train carrying young Jones to the final day of the tournament was tardy. Travis was always a stickler for punctuality and left to see the final match between Evans and Gardner.

The critical putting lesson which transformed Jones from a mediocre putter into the model of the world was postponed until 1924.

It was in the locker room of the Augusta Country Club in 1924 that Jones finally received, in the guise of a lecture, the putting lesson which changed the course of Jones' golfing history. Travis explained to Bob that he must get his feet so close together that the heels almost touch. Then he must take the club back with his left hand in a longer sweeping stroke with what appears to be hinged wrists working in opposition to each other. He changed his putting grip, overlapping the index finger of the left hand, not the right. Travis would visualize the head of a tack protruding from the back of a ball and swing the putter with the idea of driving the tack into the center of the ball. There was no sharp hit in the stroke, however. Instead it was smooth and rhythmical, with the putter swinging back and floating through against the ball.

With his new putting stroke, Jones became the Mechanical Man of Golf. In the Southern Open Championship of 1927 they *"wound up the Mechanical Man of golf and set him clicking around the East Lake Course"* in the then-record score of 66. Bob had beaten that in 1922 with a 63, but not in competition. The Mechanical Man always seemed to have a fifth gear, unknown to his opponents, but available *"on call"* whenever Bob needed it.

A vivid example of this fifth gear was presented during the 1926 Walker Cup match with Cyril Tolley. The night before the match, Jess Sweetser asked Jones, "How are you going to handle Tolley? He's the longest hitter in Great Britain and perhaps the world." Jones replied calmly, *"Jess, don't worry about Tolley."* The next day Tolley of the home team drove first. Jones then passed him about 25 yards with his first swing of the day. On the second tee Tolley hit a drive of about 275 yards and Jones again passed him. After that Tolley wasn't any factor as he continued to press to out drive Jones. The American won easily, by a record margin of 12-11.

Bob's strategy and knowledge of the rules didn't always win the day for him. He learned the power of rules decisions in 1919 at the Southern Amateur in New Orleans. On the first hole, a par 3, his ball landed in a greenskeeper's wheelbarrow and rolled into an old shoe lying inside. Instead of declaring his free drop under the *"upkeep"* rule, with which he probably didn't have the slightest familiarity, Bob elected to *"play the ball as it lies."* With a thunderous stroke he sent the shoe and its contents roaring on to the green whereupon the ball trickled out and Bob got his bogey 4 and no more. That was perhaps the last occasion upon which he failed to know the rule before playing a shot in peculiar circumstances.

He played some shots in more than peculiar circumstances — they were downright bizarre. For instance, in the Open Championship at Interlachen in 1930, Bob came to the ninth hole looking at a long spoon shot across the lake on his second shot on the par-5 hole. A couple of young girls broke as if to run across the fairway as Bob completed his backswing and started down. Bob flinched coming down and topped the shot which skidded across the pond like a young boy skipping a stone. The ball landed without disaster, and Bob capitalized on his good fortune by chipping up and making a birdie 4. It could have easily been a 7. Some spectators who saw the shot thought Jones' ball struck a lily pad in the lake which saved it from extinction. Bob scoffed at this fiction and confirmed that it was old fashioned luck at work and nothing more. *"Destiny"* was perhaps a better description.

Of course, Bob was not immune from making 7 in the crucial moments of a championship. Such was the case in the 1929 Open Championship at Winged Foot. Bob had built a 3-shot lead coming to the final round. By the eighth hole he began to feel as though the championship was in his pocket. That's also when the trouble started with a nasty bounce of the approach shot into the left greenside bunker. Bob then did what most amateurs fear in a bunker — blasting over into another bunker. From there he returned to the original bunker, and the golf began to resemble more of a tennis volley. Mercifully, the fifth stroke barely got the ball out, and with two putts he had made 7. It was ugly, but it didn't prevent Bob from tying Al Espinosa and achieving his title in the playoff. Neither did the other 7 Bob made later on the 15th hole. But that is quite another story.

Harry Vardon, the old master of golf, once expressed his opinion on the least flattering shot executed by Bob when the two were paired in the 1920 Open Championship at Toledo, Ohio. Coming to the seventh hole, both drove safely to the fairway of the short 4-par hole. Vardon hit a conservative run-up approach near the flag. Bob decided to showcase his skills in imparting backspin on the ball and attempted to hit a high niblick with lots of *"stop 'um."* He topped the shot and sculled it over the green into some bushes beyond. Until then, Vardon had been quiet as a churchmouse the entire match.

Bob broke the silence on the walk to the eighth tee. *"Mr. Vardon, did you ever see a worse shot than that?"* *"No,"* replied Vardon with a startling economy of phrase, and that was that. Soon after, Vardon accurately predicted that Jones would become the greatest player in the world.

Whereas Bob's demonstration of courage and daring went unrewarded in the Vardon match, he was blessed with the jackpot of his first major championship on the final hole of the 1923 Open playoff against wee Bobby Cruickshank. Coming to the 18th and final hole, the match was all square. Bob's drive ended in loose dirt on the edge of the right rough. Cruickshank's ball betrayed his effort at a draw into the oncoming breeze and duck hooked into the left rough. His next shot was safely played in front of a lagoon guarding the front of the green. Bob's choice was to either shoot the works with a brave stroke over the water or to play safe along with Cruickshank and engage in a duel of short games. With caution cast to the wind, Bob gambled for the green. His ball stopped seven feet to the right of the hole, and he clinched his first of four U.S. Open Championships.

There were two other strokes Bob made which were not so fortunate. In fact, they weren't even strokes at all, but they nevertheless resulted in costly penalties. In 1925, Bob played the Open at Worcester Country Club in Worcester, Massachusetts. It was so hot Bobby told Willie, *"The papers say it's over 100 degrees in the shade."* *"Yes,"* MacFarlane quipped, *"but fortunately we do not have to play in the shade."* At the 11th hole of the opening round, he addressed his ball in a heavy lie and the ball did not just rotate on its axis but moved from its original position. Only Jones could and did see it. He signaled his fault and assessed himself a penalty stroke. The USGA officials argued with Jones that the penalty was uncalled for. Bob would have none of it. There is only one way to play golf and that is by the rules. When a commentator applauded his honesty, Bob shot back disgustedly, *"You might as well praise a man for not robbing a bank!"* Some observers have emphasized that this self-inflicted penalty cost Bob the championship. While it's true Bob ended in a tie with Willie MacFarlane and lost the playoff, it is also true that Bob had ample opportunity to overcome the deficit in the latter rounds and in the playoff. Perhaps for this reason he never mentioned the episode. Just *"rub of the green."*

Another non-stroke of interest occurred in the 1926 Open Championship played at Scioto, near Columbus, Ohio. In the second round, Bob addressed his putt on the 15th green with his usual habit of first placing the putter in front of the ball to square up the blade preliminary to the actual stroke.

Unbeknownst to him, a fresh breeze was actually holding the ball steady on a slight upward grade. By placing his putter in front of the ball, Bob unwittingly blocked the force of the breeze, and the ball rolled slightly from its original position. The result was another self-inflicted penalty stroke. It did not have the apparent importance of the 1925 miscue because Bob still had to overhaul Joe Turnesa's four-shot lead in the final round. Even so, it did wonders for his reputation of unwavering integrity.

The 17th Road Hole at St. Andrews provided the setting for two other candidates which might be considered as the greatest and worst shots of Bob's golfing life.

Playing in the 1930 British Amateur against Cyril Tolley, Jones' drive was to the left of the fairway, presenting a difficult, if not impossible, approach over the villainous Road Bunker. Decades of tradition dictated that the proper play was in front of the green with the hope of an up-and-down for birdie. Eschewing tradition and using his imagination, Bob elected to play for the edge of the green nearest the 18th tee and taking the Road Bunker out of play. He signaled for the marshals to move the crowd back. When Bob's caddy finally said, *"Man, they canna move ana more,"* Bob selected his mashie 4 iron. He admittedly hit the ball a touch too strong and it ricocheted off the wall of patrons and finished on the fringe of the green. In his words, when a tough bold shot came off like that one, it was *"sheer delicatessen."* There is no better description of this stroke. Tolley got his approach up and down for a brilliant birdie 4. Bob chipped to 8 feet and hit the putt with a *"dead nerve"* into the hole for a halve. The match was decided on the 19th hole in Bob's favor with the aid of a stymie, but there is no question that Bob's play on the 17th was key to victory in the *"most important tournament"* of his life.

The difficulty of getting 4 on the Road Hole can best be illustrated by Bob's final match in 1930 against Roger Wethered. The Old Course had never been played in competition without at least one 5 on the card, or so Bob believed. As he reached the 17th, Bob had a chance to break the spell if he could only get a small four-footer down. Alas! It was not to be. Bob's victory was laced with his bitter disappointment at failure to achieve this personal goal.

He surely would have been happy with that 5 on the Road Hole in 1926 during the Walker Cup matches. Bob and Watts Gunn were partnered against Tolley and Andrew Jamieson. The latter pair found themselves in the Road on their fifth stroke, having driven out of bounds from the tee. Jones played his brassie second in proper position in front of the green, and victory seemed secure. Until the last putt goes down, however, nothing in golf is certain. Thus, Watts shanked his wee pitch into the Road in three. Jamieson then played his sixth stroke to 12 feet. Bob and Watts next put their heads together for a little strategy session. If they played for the flag, a slightly misjudged shot might find the dreaded Road Bunker and certain disaster. The safest route, back to the fairway, was chosen so that the worst score they would achieve was 7 and a sure halve. As it turned out, Tolley missed the putt and the 7 was a winner. *"But not until we had used up all our shots and most of the little brains we had,"* chuckled Bob.

In making every stroke that resulted in the greatest shot or some of the others, Jones was no doubt mindful of the wisdom offered to him by Stewart Maiden in his early years:

The idea in match golf is to get a man down, and then get him farther down. When you are one up, try to be two up on the next hole. When you have him 9 down try to get him 10 down. Play to win every hole, right up to the stage where you may be compelled to play for a halve, and then try to stick one up there for a single putt. Play for your best shot, not your safest.

Very simply, Maiden's philosophy was to give it *"all you've got"* and *"shoot the works"* on every single hole.

Years later, Keeler surveyed Jones' career to see how well he had learned the lesson:

Looking back...you may see crisis after crisis where the least slip of nerve or skill or plain fortune would have spelled...ruin. Yet at every crisis he stood up to the shot with something which I can define only as inevitability and performed what was needed with all the certainty of a natural phenomenon.

Suffice it to say, Bob hit many more good shots than bad, and his good shots were *"great"* when compared with mere mortals. Golf is the only game Bob ever knew that became harder and harder the longer anyone played it. It is perhaps for this reason that the constellation of great and not-so-great shots Bob made in his career invested in him the experience to describe the very essence of golf and its hold upon him and others:

The author appears to find it difficult to explain how golf can fix upon any person the hold of fascination that it has undeniably exerted upon many. I think I can supply some of the answers. Golf has been called "the most human of games" and a "reflection of life." One reason that we enjoy it and that it challenges us is that it enables us to run the entire gamut of human emotions, not only in a brief space of time, but likewise without measurable damage either to ourselves or to others.

***

On the golf course, a man may be the dogged victim of inexorable fate, be struck down by an appalling stroke of tragedy, become the hero of unbelievable melodrama, or the clown in a side-splitting comedy — any of these within a few hours, and all without having to bury a corpse or repair a tangled personality.

Golf may be...a sophisticated game. At least, it is usually played with the outward appearance of great dignity. It is, nevertheless, a game of considerable passion, either of the explosive type, or that which burns inwardly and sears the soul.

From his greatest shots to his worst, Bob obviously knew what he was talking about.

Chapter 12
Off the Course:
Recreation and
Relaxation

As a retired lawyer and businessman, Bob Jones was able to enjoy his hobbies, which included non-tournament golf.

A great many people have asked me how it feels to be through with competitive golf to find myself joined to the ranks of the has-beens who look on from the sidelines where no one bothers much about them. Some of these people seem to think that a competitive sports career in this day and time is not an easy thing to give up. Certainly it would be a difficult thing for me if my retirement from competition necessarily meant that I should be giving up golf entirely. What I look forward to now is what I have conceived to be the real way to enjoy golf. To play a lot, never too seriously; to go to all the tournaments in the role of spectator; to play a few rounds in practice with the boys, and then sit back and watch, and perhaps write a little stuff if anyone wants to read it; to study the mechanics of the game, to experiment without fear of disturbing my swing before a championship; to play in charity matches and minor tournaments if and whenever I like, but always to leave the big ones to those who are willing to take the punishment.

From his youth, Bob enjoyed playing baseball. His father, Colonel Jones, played for the University of Georgia and signed a contract to play with the Brooklyn Superbas of the National League. But "R.T." Jones (Bob's grandfather) would have none of it and demanded that his son go to law school. When he was 5, Bob was astonished to see an organ grinder who had a monkey so skillful at catching a ball that Bob envied him.

Indeed, I had a hazy wish to be a monkey and astonish the boys at my skill at catching the ball. In those days I used to catch behind the bat without a mask — our appliances were limited — and was rather proud of the position, which was regarded as dangerous. One day Bob Ravenel swung too hard at a pitched ball, the bat came all the way around, slipped out of his hands, and cracked me on the side of the head. I ceased to be a hero at once; I never went behind the plate again.

Bob later became a director of the "Atlanta Crackers" of the Southern Association. The umpire in this photo is L.W. Robert, president of the club. The catcher is R.L. Spiller, an owner and club official.

Tennis with Bob Jones at Highlands, anyone?
Bob takes to the courts at Highlands Country Club,
Highlands, N.C. on August 27, 1933.

First National Bank of Chicago President Melvin Traylor and Bob Jones posed for the camera with a lot of "birdies." In 1928, as president of the USGA, Melvin Traylor presented the National Amateur Championship cup to Bob at Brae Burn. Traylor was also sitting in the front row when Bob received the last of his four Grand Slam trophies at Merion. Thereafter, Traylor was a founding member of the Augusta National Golf Club. Traylor was one of the handful of bankers who accurately predicted in early 1929 the onset of the Great Depression and even warned Clifford Roberts in time to protect himself and his clients. Traylor was the initial vice-president of Augusta National.

Bob and Mary Jones out for a ride together. One day, as Jones was out riding, he was stopped by Judge Robert Bingham, United States ambassador to the Court of St. James in London. The U.S. ambassador looked at Mr. Jones and said, *"You are the greatest ambassador to England that America has ever had."*

The "Boys Club" at Highlands C.C. One of the cabins to the left of the fourth green was a gathering place, from time to time, of (from the left) Morton Hodgson, Bob Jones, R.W. Woodruff, and Clifford Roberts. Bob once reflected:

Quite honestly, I have no longing for the 'old cheers, loud and free.' I had my day long ago and I am quite content now to applaud with the other spectators. But the wonderful thing about golf is that it holds forever the interest of all who play it; and so I find myself today a member of a sort of fraternity of those who walk the fairways with me, with numbers considerably augmented by the many who have come since...The championships have been very much worth the effort they cost, but more important by far have been the expanding interests they brought and the avenues to friendships with individuals and groups of people they opened for me. That these rewards should endure so long makes it easy to see why for me golf will always be the greatest game.

Bob Jones' luck at fishing was pretty good, too. When Bob became immobilized with the spinal disease, close friend Charlie Elliott constructed a special fishing boat for Bob featuring a chair which swiveled 360 degrees. As Bob was lifted into the boat on one trip, the dock worker said, *"It is amazing that a man in your crippled condition could have been such a great golfer."* Bob Jones simply chuckled and said, *"It wasn't easy."*

On August 15, 1948, Bob played his last round with (from left) Bob Ingram, Tommy Barnes, and Henry Lindner. Charlie Yates recalled, *"I also recall quite vividly and sadly how one day in 1948 we were crossing the bridge on the island hole and Bob said that he had trouble getting the club down from the top of his swing because of the pain in his back. 'I guess I won't be playing with you boys anymore for a while,' Bob said, 'I've decided to have an operation.' Of course, he never played with us again."*

Chapter 13
Building
Augusta National

Bob Jones met Clifford Roberts in the mid '20s through a mutual friend, Walton H. Marshal, who ran the Vanderbilt Hotel in New York and the Bon Air Vanderbilt Hotel in Augusta, Georgia. Bob and his dad, Col. R.P. Jones, frequently stayed in Marshal's hotels, both in New York and Augusta. Roberts was an eyewitness to Bob's second hole-in-one at the Augusta Country Club on January 13, 1932, on the 14th hole, which measured 145 yards. Jones used a 4 iron. In the fall of 1930, Roberts suggested to Bob in a 10-minute conversation that Augusta was the logical place to build Jones' *"ideal golf course."* An option was obtained at a price of $70,000 for the Fruitlands Nurseries.

The clubhouse of Augusta National Golf Club was initially built in 1854 by Dennis Redmond and was supposed to be the first cement house constructed in the South. Redmond purchased an initial 315 acres of land on Washington Road and named it "Fruitlands." An additional 50 acres were added, and the property was operated as an indigo plantation. It was purchased in 1857 by a Belgian baron, Louis Mathieu Edouard Berckmans. Berckmans was an ardent horticulturist, and he *"indulged his hobby to the limit of his resources."* When Jones first laid eyes upon it, he remarked, *"Perfect! And to think this ground has been lying here all these years waiting for someone to come along and lay a golf course upon it."*

Dr. ALISTER MACKENZIE
GOLF ARCHITECT
105 W. Monroe St.   604 Federal Reserve   331 Madison Ave.
Chicago   Bank Bldg.   New York
             San Francisco

Bob Jones invited Dr. Alister MacKenzie to work with him in designing Augusta National. *"No man learns to design a golf course simply by playing golf, no matter how well,"* Bob said in making this judgment. Jones had met MacKenzie in 1929 when Bob was defeated in the first round of the Amateur by Johnny Goodman and was thereafter invited to play Cypress Point, designed by MacKenzie. Alister MacKenzie was a medical doctor who had learned the clever art of camouflage during the Boer War in South Africa. He used the same techniques in designing golf courses built for the *"most enjoyment for the greatest number."*

Alister MacKenzie (second from left) watches Bob Jones drive from a proposed location of the eighth tee during construction of the course. MacKenzie had an uncommon instinct of knowing where *"to cut a vista through the woods so as to expose an unusually beautiful view."* Bob explained the importance of this exercise:

There are two ways of widening the gap between a good tee shot and a bad one. One is to inflict a severe and immediate punishment on a bad shot, to place its perpetrator in a bunker or in some other trouble which will demand the sacrifice of a stroke in recovering. The other is to reward the good shot by making the second shot simpler in proportion to the excellence of the first. The reward may be of any nature, but it is more commonly one of four — a better view of the green, an easier angle from which to attack a slope, an open approach past guarding hazards, or even a better run to the tee shot itself. But the elimination of purely punitive hazards provides an opportunity for the player to retrieve his situation by an exceptional second shot.

Jones and MacKenzie survey Fruitlands Nursery with prospective members. (From the left) Dr. Alister MacKenzie; Charles Grace, son of Eugene Grace, president of Bethlehem Steel Corporation; Bobby Jones; Eugene Grace; and Devereux Milburn, noted polo player. MacKenzie acknowledged the significant contributions which Jones made to the Augusta National design:

Bob (as his intimates call him) regularly collaborated with me during the months of architectural designing. He rendered me assistance of incalculable value. I am convinced that from no one else could I have obtained such help. Bob is not only a student of golf, but of golf courses as well, and while I had known him for years, I was amazed at his knowledge and clear recollection of almost all of the particularly famous golf holes in England and Scotland as well as America.

***

Bobby is not only the President of the Club, but is the active leader in all matters pertaining to designing, construction and organization. He assumes the major responsibility in this effort to build 'the ideal golf course.'

ROBERT TYRE JONES, JR.
ATLANTA, GEORGIA

September 2, 1931

Mr. Crawford Johnson
Birmingham, Alabama

Dear Crawford:

You may have heard that I am interested
with a group of friends in organizing a new golf
club in Augusta, Georgia.   The enclosed preliminary
draft of the invitation will tell you something about
it.

What I want to accomplish there is an ideal
golf club, with every facility for golf, including a
course which will be outstanding.   Dr. Alister Mac
Kenzie, the architect in charge, and I have spent two
days together on the property and we both believe that
we can do just that.

I am particularly anxious to interest my own
friends in this project to get them to come down and
play the course and take an interest in the club.   I
am therefore writing you to ask if you will not join
this club and serve on it's board of governors.   I
know you can be of assistance to us in getting the kind
of members we want.

Please be assured that you will not be asked
for any financial assistance other than the cost of a
membership.   A sufficient sum has been underwritten by
people interested in Augusta and the south to enable us
to complete the construction of the course and the modest clubhouse which we intend to build.   The whole
story is that I have an opportunity to build a golf
course according to my own ideas at a place which I deem
ideally situated, and I want to have the right people
associated with me in running it.

If you don't feel that the thing would appeal
to you, please feel perfectly free to say so.   My own
thought is that I should like to have you if you think
you would enjoy it.   I will be most happy to supply
additional information if you would like to have it.

With warmest regards,

most sincerely,

Bob Jones

Robert Tyre Jones, Jr.

Captains of industry at Augusta. After the property had been secured, Jones and Roberts began to build a national membership for the club which Bob named "Augusta National Golf Club." Although it was the height of the depression, sufficient founding members were invited to join during golf outings such as this one. Pictured are (seated left to right): Rex Cole, president of the Rex Cole Refrigerator Corp.; M.H. Aylesworth, president of the National Broadcasting Company; Bobby Jones; Kent Cooper, general manager of the Associated Press; W.A. Jones, chairman of the Executive Committee of Henry L. Doherty & Co. (Standing left to right) Richard C. Patterson, Jr., Commissioner of Corrections of New York City; John W. Harris of Hegeman-Harris Co., builders of Radio City; Dr. Alister MacKenzie; Grantland Rice; Alfred Severin Bourne, Singer sewing machine magnate; Fielding Wallace; and Clifford Roberts.

The course was completed in December 1932. The elaborate result included 80 acres of fairway, 100,000 square feet of greens, and an additional 16,000 square feet of collars around the greens. Even after construction of the course, Bob Jones' thrill of seeing it for the first time did not diminish:

I shall never forget my first visit to the property which is now the Augusta National. The long lane of magnolias through which we approached was beautiful. The old manor house with its cupola and walls of masonry two feet thick was charming. The rare trees and shrubs of the old nursery were enchanting. But when I walked out on the grass terrace under the big trees behind the house and looked down over the property, the experience was unforgettable...Indeed, it even looked as though it were already a golf course, and I am sure that one standing today where I stood on this first visit, on the terrace overlooking the practice putting green, sees the property almost exactly as I saw it then...I still like to sit on this terrace and can do so for hours at a time, enjoying the beauty of this panorama.

Before distinguished golf writer Herbert Warren Wind named *"Amen Corner,"* it still provided much excitement for those who played it 20 years earlier on opening day.

During the construction of the third green (now the 12th), workers discovered the presence of an Indian burial ground. A wooden bridge connected the third tee with the green located 120 yards away. Gold was also discovered during the construction of the course, although laboratory tests showed it was not rich enough for mining purposes.

Bob Jones watches his playing partner putt on the fourth green (now the 13th). Unlike today, Rae's Creek was visible from the clubhouse.

The tee for the fourth hole (now the 13th) was located close to Rae's Creek - a championship distance of 440 yards. In the background is the fairway of the second hole (now the 11th).

Bob Jones tees off on the first hole (now the 10th) of the First Annual Invitation Tournament in March 1934. Bob was excited that championship-caliber golf could finally be played in the South. *"I must confess that the prospect of annually entertaining my old playmates and the later arrivals in the upper crust of competitive golf was quite attractive."* When Clifford Roberts initially suggested that the tournament be called the *"Masters,"* Bob thought *"the name was borne of a touch of immodesty."* But by 1938, he acquiesced. *"I think the tournament is quite well entitled to be called the Masters because it has continued to assemble those who are entitled to be called the masters of the game."*

Bob Jones putting on the eighth green during the third round of the 1935 Annual Invitational Tournament in which Bob carded a total of 219, 10 strokes behind Craig Wood. In this same tournament, Gene Sarazen hit the shot *"heard round the world"* when his No. 4 wood launched the ball into the hole for a double eagle on No. 15. Sarazen tied Wood and beat him the following day in a playoff.

The 1935 Masters Field. This photograph has been often mistaken as the inaugural 1934 tournament. An often-published copy of this photograph contains the signature of most of the players. Several of the players who were not present for this original photograph were later "dubbed" in, including Walter Hagen, Horton Smith, Leo Diegel and Errie Ball. *Back Row:* Phil Perkins, George Jacobus, Byron Nelson, Al Espinosa, Jug McSpaden, Denny Shute, Freddie Haas, Al Watrous, Gene Kunes, Dick Metz, Willie Klein, John Dawson, Jack Munger, Wilford Wehrle,

Gus Moreland, Ky Laffoon, Ralph Stonehouse. *Center Row:* Andy Kay, Tommy Armour, Jules Hout, Bill Schwartz, Bill Mehlhorn, Freddie McLeod, Jock Hutchison, Frank Walsh, Craig Wood, Ray Mangrum, Clarence Clark, Jimmy Hines, Mike Turnesa, Joe Turnesa, Vic Ghezzi, Abe Espinosa, Walter Kozak, Pat Tiso. *Front Row:* Jimmy Foulis, Tony Manero, Bobby Cruickshank, Gene Sarazen, Charlie Yates, Paul Runyan, Bobby Jones, Olin Dutra, Johnny Farrell, Willie MacFarlane, Jimmy Thomson, Harry Cooper, Johnny Revolta, Henry Picard.

After his playing days were over, Bob still continued his important role as host. In this photo, Bob reminisces with the Duke of Windsor, perhaps about the grand match they had on the estate of Sir Phillip Sassoon near Trent in 1930. It was part of an outing with the Oxford Cambridge Golfing Society and the U.S. Walker Cup Team.

The Augusta National president in perpetuity, Bob Jones sits in the special golf cart provided to him when he became immobile. Bob seen welcoming President Eisenhower at Augusta. In 1956, at an Augusta National Club governors meeting, Eisenhower announced, in a most serious vain, that the chief torment and concern of his life was the big pine tree located in the left center of the 17th fairway. He stated that it *"acted as a magnet to his drive. No matter where he aimed, he always hit this tree. The President went on to demand that the offending tree be chopped down forthwith."* At that point Cliff Roberts decided that the only way to protect the Club's property would be to declare the meeting adjourned which he did.

Jack Nicklaus and Bob Jones visit during one of the last occasions on which Jones was able to make it to the Masters. (1968 was his last year.) Jones said of Nicklaus: *"He plays a game with which I am not familiar."* Nicklaus said of Jones:

My first golf hero was Bob Jones, and this of course was a fortunate thing...I have learned an awful lot from him...In a word he has embodied the spirit of golf.

On the ship going to the 1936 Olympic Games in Berlin, Jones was persuaded by R.W. Woodruff to stop in Gleneagles, Scotland, for a few days of golf. While there, Jones said, *"I could not leave here without playing at St. Andrews. Of all the courses I have played in this country, I think St. Andrews is the best, and it is worth the trip across the Atlantic to visit it once more."* A chauffeur was dispatched to enter the name "R.T. Jones, Jr." on a ballot for tee time on the Old Course. While having lunch overlooking the first tee, Bob noticed 2,000 St. Andreans had lined the fairways. He feared that his informal match had been scheduled during an important tournament. Actually, word had spread like wildfire throughout the *"Auld Grey Toon"* of Jones' match, and the entire town turned out to see it while placing signs in their shops: *"Bobby's back."*

Bob noticed that *"there was a sort of holiday mood in the crowd. It seemed, or they made it appear at least, that they were just glad to see me back, and however I chose to play golf was all right with them, only that they wanted to see it."* Standing next to Bob's wife, Mary, and Grantland Rice was a Scot who had tears streaming down his cheeks, *"Isn't it graund...isn't it graund...Bobby's back."*

Bob's original match was quickly recast to include (from left) Gordon Lockhart, the Gleneagles Hotel professional, and Willie Auchterlone, R&A club professional and 1893 Open Champion. On the far right is Provost Boase, Captain of the R&A. The players had to wait 20 minutes before they could play off, and during that time, Bob Jones had to face a battery of cameras. *"Scores of people invaded the first teeing ground and fairway, and as they could be persuaded by friendly shouts to stand clear to give the players room to swing a club, three green rangers and a number of R&A members and others who volunteered their services as stewards, proceeded to induce them to form an avenue wide enough to allow the players to make a start."*

Only once was Jones off-line from the tee, and his approach shots were marvels of accuracy. He started the fireworks at the second where he holed a 12-yard putt for a birdie 3. He parred the next three holes and then secured another birdie 3 at the fifth hole. On the par-3 eighth hole, Jones played a softly fading No. 4 iron and stopped his ball only three yards from the hole giving him a birdie 2. As he gently slipped his club back in the bag, Bob's caddy whispered to him, *"My, but you're a wonder, sir."*

Bob played the outward half in 32. *"I was so happy and in a transport almost that when I reached the 11th, I went over Strath going for the green and landed in a bunker that no longer exists. It was about 15 feet from the hole, and I went out looking for that bunker the other day, and the greenskeeper told me it had never been there. I said to him — 'You can't tell me that, because I played two shots in it in 1936,"* Bob explained years later. No one seemed to care about Bob's inward half of 40. There were loud cheers and hardy applause when Mr. Jones holed his 8-yard putt for a birdie 3 at the home hole. As soon as the other players had holed out, the sanctity of the famous Tom Morris turf was violated by hundreds of the spectators, who rushed across to where Mr. Jones was standing. The former champion was besieged by autograph hunters, but he managed to make his way to the R&A Clubhouse, where he found refuge. He was anxious not to disappoint his admirers, and those who desired his autograph were lined up on one side of the entrance to the Clubhouse and allowed to pass through the portico where Mr. Jones obliged with his signature. He signed scores of books, papers, and postcards, and even appended his signature to cigarette packets and novels before he called a halt.

Jones' extensive formal education served him well in the prolific writings he authored during his lifetime. Not a single ghostwriter assisted Bob in writing over a half-million words in the hundreds of newspaper columns written for the Bell Syndicate from 1927 until 1935. Bob also wrote four books and occasional articles for the *American Golfer* magazine.

In 1950, the Associated Press conducted a 50-year poll of the sportswriters and sports broadcasters who confirmed that Bob Jones was the greatest golfer of the half century. A 1952 PGA poll also voted Jones the top amateur golfer of the half century.

RICHARD NIXON

September 15, 1993

577 CHESTNUT RIDGE ROAD
WOODCLIFF LAKE, NEW JERSEY

Mr. Sidney L. Matthew
Gorman & Matthew, P.A.
135 South Monroe Street
Suite 100
Tallahassee, Florida   32302

Dear Mr. Matthew:

I believe that the photograph you enclosed with your letter of August 26th was taken at a lunch or dinner at The Plaza Hotel honoring Bobby Jones.

I remember that as one who was just beginning to play golf, I felt particularly privileged to sit between Bobby and Jack Nicklaus.

I recall very little about what I said on that occasion, except that I remember Bobby got a big kick out of my relating the problem I had in determining what to have for lunch before going out for a round of golf. I said that I had tried everything. I had tried having a big lunch, a small lunch and no lunch - and nothing helped. Then one day I played with Tommy Armour. I had what he had for lunch, and I couldn't even see the ball!

Bobby made an enormous impression on me, as he did on everyone who was privileged to know him personally. In addition to being an extraordinarily gifted athelete, he was a fine Southern gentleman.

Sincerely,

Richard Nixon

In January 1960, Jones presented the Metropolitan Golfwriters Gold Tee Award to Francis Ouimet. On that occasion, Jones received from Vice President Richard M. Nixon, a special trophy commemorating the 30th anniversary of the Grand Slam.

Chapter 15
The War Years

On June 9, 1942, Jones was commissioned a captain in the Army Air Force. With a medical disability and at age 40, being beyond the active service age for recruits, Jones was not compelled to go to war. But he signed up anyway saying, *"I'm very happy over this opportunity to serve. I had been looking around to see what I could do and about a month ago sent in my application. I am very glad that it has come through and I am anxious to get going."*

Jones landed at Normandy on the day after D-Day where he spent two months in the line of fire. Shortly before he returned home, Bob enjoyed a USO entertainment program only miles from enemy lines. In August 1944, Jones was discharged as a lieutenant-colonel.

Chapter 16
Freedom of the Royal Burgh of St. Andrews

The transatlantic plane which carried Bob and Mary Jones (above) and the American team made an emergency landing in Newfoundland after losing an engine. President Eisenhower said of Jones:

Those who have been fortunate enough to know Bob Jones realize that his fame as a golfer is transcended by his inestimable qualities as a human being. Bob's contribution to our great game is reflected by its deserved prominence in the field of sports, but his gift to his friends is the warmth that comes from unselfishness, superb judgment, nobility of character and unwavering loyalty of principle.

"It is a wonderful experience to go about a town where people wave at you from doorways and windows, where strangers smile and greet you by name, often your first name, and where a simple and direct courtesy is the outstanding characteristic," Bob later wrote of his visit with the people in St. Andrews.

Bob was deeply impressed with the sensitivity of the people of St. Andrews and their ability to extend cordiality in an ingenious way. *"Friends are a man's priceless treasures, and a life rich in friendship is full indeed,"* was one way Bob expressed his feelings. He eschewed using his friends to enrich himself saying, *"You can only eat two eggs in the morning. You can only wear one suit a day. All you need is enough to stay even and be decent to your friends."*

Prior to presenting the silver casket containing the scroll to Bob Jones, Provost Leonard said, *"We welcome him for his own sake; we welcome him also as an ambassador in the cause of international understanding and good will which the competition of this week is designed to promote. We welcome him moreover not only as a distinguished golfer but as a man of outstanding character, courage, and accomplishment well worthy to adorn the Roll of our Honorary Burgesses."*

As Provost Leonard presented the silver casket to Bob Jones, he smiled broadly, and with a twinkle in his eye set Jones at ease saying, *"Now, Bob, the ordeal is yours."* Jones recalled later, *"Within the few seconds it took me to make my way to the lectern along the table so thoughtfully provided, I found out how a man's life, or a great part of it, can flash through his mind in an instant. I knew in that instant that I had no need for the notes in my pocket. I knew that I would have no difficulty finding things to say to the people of St. Andrews."*

One reporter in Younger Hall wrote:

The occasion could have been a mere formality but for Bobby, who spoke with such simplicity and feeling that everyone was aware what a really great man they had in their midst.

Perhaps the most memorable and often quoted statement Bob made was, *"I could take out of my life everything except my experiences at St. Andrews and I would still have a rich full life."*

Next morning, almost completely crippled now, he was driven out on to the Old Course in the same electric buggy — the first, I believe, ever to be seen at St. Andrews — and once again huge crowds assembled to wish him well. And who was privileged to drive him on that occasion? Well, it was me. A proud experience, indeed, remarked Henry Longhurst.

Chapter 18
Memorials to One Hero

GAME CALLED — DARKNESS. On December 18, 1971, golfers on the Old Course stopped their play as the flag on the clubhouse was lowered to half staff in front of the 18th hole. News had been received that Bobby Jones was gone.

ROBERT TYRE JONES, JR.
MARCH 17, 1902
DECEMBER 18, 1971

MARY MALONE JONES
JULY 24, 1902
MAY 23, 1975

Leaden gray skies turned Atlanta into a symbolic reminder of the "Auld Grey Toon" on the day Bob Jones was put to rest in Atlanta's historic Oakland Cemetery on December 20, 1971. Only his family and a few close friends attended the short service which was devoid of elaborate eulogies. Even so, a symphony of tributes echoed throughout the world.

A further historic tribute was made on September 10, 1972, when the St. Andrews town council named the 10th hole on the Old Course the *"Bobby Jones"* hole. The 10th hole was the only one unnamed; the only other hole named for a golfer was the 18th being the famous *"Tom Morris"* hole. (From the left) The Rev. W. Rankin, chaplain to the Royal & Ancient Golf Club; Councillor James Thomson, and Provost David Niven.

*"When the One Great Scorer comes to write
against your name, he marks not that you won
or lost, but how you played The Game"*
Grantland Rice

ACKNOWLEDGMENTS

Initially, the author must confess, the many hours spent on this project have been purloined from the reservoir earmarked for his wife and family. To Linda, Lauren, and Geoffrey, this endeavor has been known affectionately as the author's *"ultimate obsession,"* especially in light of the fact that even the playing of golf has been forsaken as its consequence. For Jennifer, Jeff, and grandson Skylar, it is hoped that the mere completion of this work will yield some relief and opportunity to exhale at last.

The author is certainly indebted to Robert Tyre Jones IV, Bob Jones' grandson, for his gracious foreword and no less for his friendship and help in separating the wheat from the chaff.

Another note of genuine appreciation must be extended posthumously to Clara Jones Black, Bob Jones' eldest child.

It is right and proper to extend the author's profound gratitude to Joseph S.F. Murdoch and Bob Kuntz, co-founders of the Golf Collectors Society, for encouragement and valuable assistance in such a task as this.

Among the private collectors who have generously and unselfishly offered images in their collections, are Kiltie Leach (grandson of Stewart Maiden), James C. "Cam" Maiden (son of Jimmy Maiden), George Keeler (son of O.B. Keeler), Paul Ackerly (grandnephew of Eleanor McIntosh Keeler), Mary Ella Ackerly, Jim Pruitt, Sr. and Jim Pruitt, Jr., David R. Clark, Bud Duffner, George and Ann Thomas, Chris Coon, Dave Berkowitz, Bob Fernbacher, Dennis Levine, Dr. David Aldrich, Tom Steinhardt, Ray Davis, Jim Tingley, Charles Brett, Jim Long, Jim Santy, Jim Knerr, Hank Alperin, Retired USGA Museum Curator Janet Seagle, Dick Gordin, Walter Wattles, Doug Campbell, Dick Murphy, Rusty Higgins, Brian Siplo, John W. Fischer III (son of the last person to win a major championship with hickory shafts being the 1936 Amateur), Mark Emerson, Bill Anderson, Dr. Bill Bridges, Cliff Campbell, W.P. Westbrook, Bob Wooldridge, Steve Willadsen, Dick Donovan, and Gus Sissom.

Certain clubs and museums have also contributed mightily in supplying needed data including Augusta National Golf Club (Jim Armstrong, Barbara Spenser), the USGA, Karen Bednarski, R&A Golf Club of St. Andrews, (Michael Bonallack) St. Andrews Golf Club (of which the author is a proud member), Highlands CC (Walter Wattles, Doug Campbell, Carroll Peacock), Atlanta Athletic Club (Bill O'Callaghan, Chris Borders, Eugene Branch), James River CC & Museum (Weymouth Crumpler), East Lake GC (Tom Cousins), Sigma Alpha Epsilon Fraternity (Chris Coon), Atlanta History Center, High Museum, Woodruff Arts Center of Atlanta, Emory University (Linda Matthews and Kathy Knox), Richard Nixon Library at Yorba Linda, California, Dwight D. Eisenhower Library at Abilene, Kansas, St. Andrews Scotland University Library (Robert Smart, Keeper of Muniments), Warner Bros. Studios and Archives (Leith Adams), Bettman Archives, Wide World Photos, and FPA Studios. Thanks also to the Chick Evans Foundation (Gary Holloway) for their cooperation. Bud Duffner, publisher of Golfiana, provided needed editorial help and supplied important images.

The author is indebted to Jonesheirs, Inc. (Arthur Howell, Esq. and Marty Elgison, Esq.) for their courtesy and kindness in facilitating various needed permissions. Other knowledgeable and selfless contributors to the instant endeavor include F.R. *"Bobby"* Furber, Ray Davis, past curator of the PGA Hall of Fame Museum and Morton and John Olman, the old Tom Morris and young Tom Morris of golf collecting, Bob Jones' law partner, Eugene Branch, Tommy Barnes, Charlie Elliott, Watts Gunn, Mrs. Jane Gunn, Morton S. Hodgson, Errie Ball, Woodrow Bryant, Dan Yates, Charlie and Dorothy Yates.

Production and essential editing herein have been contributed by Rowland Publishing, Inc. (Brian Rowland, President) Steven Leukanech, Scott Brightwell and Charles Vorce.

Thanks to the design/layout/production genius of Scott (The Hammer) Willis, Buddy (The Blade) Walker and Howell (The Deuce) Tucker of Grand AD Graphics & Design of Tallahassee.

Lastly, in order to give special emphasis, the author expresses his profound thanks to his loyal and highly competent legal staff. Gwynne Chason, P.L.S., with 18 years of loyal service; Mavis Cooksey, retired after 10 years; and Cindy Thompson, veteran of 10 years in the law,

To God be the Glory.

PHOTO CREDITS

80   Gus B. Sissom
81   Gus B. Sissom
82   SLM Collection
83   SLM Collection
84   SLM Collection
85   Western Golf Association
86   Western Golf Association
87   Emory
88   SLM Collection
89   Atlanta Journal
90   American Golfer/SLM Collection
91   Western Golf Association
92   David R. Clark
93   Western Golf Association
94   Emory
95   Emory
96   Emory
97   SLM Collection
98   American Sports Publishing Company/SLM Collection
99   Tom Steinhardt
100 SLM Collection
101 Hulton Deutsch Collection
102 Emory
103 Hulton Deutsch Collection
104 Mid-Week Pictorial/NYT Pictures
105 Mid-Week Pictorial/NYT Pictures
106 Emory
107 Mid-Week Pictorial/NYT Pictures

108 Western Golf Association/Emory
109 American Sports Publishing Company/SLM Collection
110 Emory
111 SLM Collection
112 Emory
113 SLM Collection
114 SLM Collection
115 SLM Collection
116 Mid-Week Pictorial/NYT Pictures
117 Atlanta Journal
130 American Sports Publishing Company/SLM Collection
131 SLM Collection
132 United States Golf Association (USGA)
133 USGA
134 Emory
135 SLM Collection
136 SLM Collection
137 SLM Collection
138 SLM Collection
139 Dundee Courier
140 SLM Collection
141 Emory
142 SLM Collection
143 Mid-Week Pictorial/NYT Pictures
144 SLM Collection
145 Emory
146 David Berkowitz

PHOTO CREDITS

147 Times Wide World Photos/NYT

148 Times Wide World Photos/NYT

149 Jim Pruitt

150 SLM Collection

151 David Berkowitz

152 SLM Collection

153 SLM Collection

154 SLM Collection

155 SLM Collection

156 SLM Collection

157 Jim Pruitt

158 SLM Collection

159 USC Library/Hearst

160 David Berkowitz

161 UPI Bettmann

162 Jim Pruitt

164 Eugene Branch

165 Atlanta Athletic Club

166 NYT Pictures

167 The High Museum

168 Bud Duffner

169 Frank Christian [Royal Liverpool Golf Club]

170 Sunningdale Golf Club

171 Atlanta History Center

172 SLM Collection

173 SLM Collection

174 Times Wide World Photos/NYT Pictures

175 Time, Inc. Publications

176 SLM Collection

177 SLM Collection

178 SLM Collection

179 Copyright 1994 United States Golf Association and Robert Walker

180 Copyright 1994 United States Golf Association and Robert Walker

181 Copyright 1994 United States Golf Association and Robert Walker

182 Times Wide World Photos/NYT Pictures

183 (Top) USGA (Bottom) Augusta National Golf Club

184 Atlanta History Center; J. Hixson Kinsella

185 Highlands Country Club

186 Emory

187 (Top) Atlanta Athletic Club (Bottom) Atlanta Athletic Club

188 Time, Inc. Publications

189 Augusta National Golf Club

190 (Top) Charlie Elliott (Bottom) Emory

191 (a,b,c) SLM Collection (d) SAE

192 (a) Golfing Magazine (b) Golf World Magazine (c) Golf Magazine (d) Golf Magazine

193 (a) SLM Collection (b) Georgia Golf Magazine (c) Georgia Magazine (d) Tom Steinhardt

194 (a) Doubleday & Company
(b) Winston, Holt & Reinhart
(c) Bob Jones, IV
(d) Chatto & Windus
195 Augusta National Golf Club
196 Emory
214 American Sports Publishing Company/SLM Collection
215 SLM Collection
216 USC Library/Hearst
217 Jim Pruitt
218 USC Library/Hearst
219 SLM Collection
220 Emory
221 George Eastman House
222 American Golfer
236 Emory
237 USC Library/Hearst
238 FPG International
239 Emory
240 Emory
241 FPG International
242 Emory
243 Emory
244 Jim Pruitt
245 Tommy Barnes
248 Mark Emerson
249 Western Golf Association
250 Western Golf Association
251 Western Golf Association
252 Western Golf Association
253 Crawford Johnson, Jr.

254 Emory
256 FPG International
257 Western Golf Association
258 Wide World Photos/NYT Pictures
259 SLM Collection
260 Frank Christian
261 Frank Christian
264 Atlanta Journal and Constitution
265 Frank Christian
266 Frank Christian
267 St. Andrews University
268 St. Andrews University
269 St. Andrews University
270 SLM Collection
271 St. Andrews University
272 Atlanta History Center
273 USC Library/Hearst
274 SLM Collection
275 Emory
278 Emory
279 Emory
282 Pan American
283 (Top) St. Andrews University
(Bottom) SLM Collection
284 St. Andrews University
285 Dundee Courier
286 Golf Magazine, Sept. 1960, p. 66
288 Emory
289 SLM Collection
290 Dundee Courier
291 SLM Collection
Back Endleaf SLM Collection